*Batter Up* is an inspiring book ... baseball fans. James Walters's ... demonstrate his love of fatherhood and baseball. You will find in this book an invitation to live your calling as a father with greater joy and passion.

> **Bobby Valentine**, Former MLB Player and Manager

*Batter Up* is a celebration of baseball and fatherhood. On the summer when my father, Gil Hodges, is enshrined in Cooperstown, this book invites all fathers to live a Hall of Fame life for their children.

> **Gil Hodges Jr.**, Executive Director Gil Hodges
> Organization for Children & Families

Dr Jimmy Walters's book *Batter Up* puts faith, fatherhood and baseball in the proper perspective. I encourage everyone to read this book.

> **Ed Blankmeyer**, Current Chicago Cubs
> Minor League Coach and former St. John's University
> Hall of Fame Head Coach

To me, as a former baseball player and father to two sons, Walters's book really hits home. This book is a wonderful reminder of the importance of family and faith and gives a great perspective on what should be prioritized in your daily life.

> **Ed Kull**, Director of Intercollegiate Athletics
> and Recreational Sports & Sr. Executive Director
> of Development, Fordham University

Whether you are a fan of baseball or any other sport, *Batter Up* by Dr. James Walters provides busy fathers with the inspiration to slow down and recommit to the vocation of fatherhood.

> **Mike St. Pierre**, Executive Director,
> Campus Ministry Association

Baseball is synonymous with religion. After all, the first words in the Bible are "In the beginning." Baseball is America's great secular religion. It reflects who we are and what we aspire to be. Faith is the heartbeat of every baseball fan. Every father who has handed down baseball to the next generation owes Jimmy Walters a debt of gratitude for this love letter to them and to his God. The timing of this book for our troubled world is impeccable.

**Ed Randall**, Host, "Remember When," Sirius/XM Radio

James Walters's account of the emotional and spiritual revelations of fatherhood is a must-read for anyone nurturing a young life. Drawing from both his personal experience as a dad and the wisdom of Catholic figures past and present, Walters invites fathers and fathers-to-be to live into this heart-expanding time, fully embracing the joys and challenges of this important vocation.

**Jennifer Sawyer**, Editor-in-Chief of Busted Halo

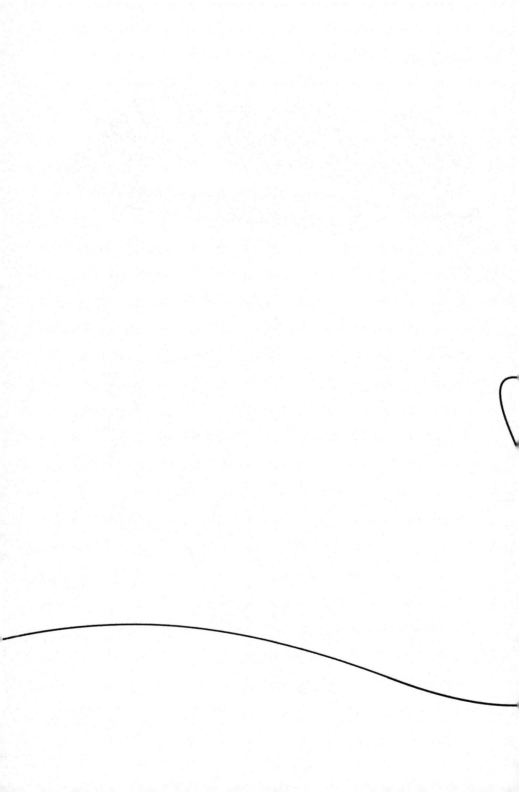

# Batter Up

## Answering the Call of
## Faith & Fatherhood

# James R. Walters

**New City Press**
Hyde Park, New York

To my Amazin' teammate, Suzie,
To my All-Stars, Shea & Lily,
and to my Hall of Fame parents, Annette & Jim.

Published by New City Press
202 Comforter Blvd.,
Hyde Park, NY 12538
www.newcitypress.com

Batter Up
Answering the Call of Faith & Fatherhood

James R. Walters

Cover design and layout by Miguel Tejerina

Library of Congress Control Number: 2022933900

ISBN: 978-1-56548-537-2 (Paperback)
ISBN: 978-1-56548-604-1 (E-book)

Printed in the United States of America

# Contents

# Introduction

In Cooperstown, New York, you find the home of Major League Baseball's Hall of Fame. Hundreds of thousands flock there annually to remember the greatest one percent who ever played the game, their attention focused on images of these baseball giants captured on bronze plaques. Over four thousand miles away and across the Atlantic Ocean, a different kind of pilgrims journey to St. Peter's Basilica in Vatican City. Here, they encounter precious art depicting some of the most exemplary holy individuals who ever lived. The Hall of Fame and St. Peter's Basilica, as well as the many other secular and sacred pilgrimage sites across the globe, invite wayfarers not only to stand in awe of greatness, but also to consider their own magnificence.

Although excelling in a game and skill does not compare to living and reflecting God's love, on and off the field our baseball icons have brought together people, lifted spirits, and inspired hope. The great saints reveal unique paths to holiness that go beyond reverence for a marble statue on a pedestal. Their lives call us to look within and to ponder how we are leaving our mark on this world, and those we accompany on our shared journey.

While I will never be enshrined in Cooperstown or have a halo drawn over my greying hair, I am, like you, called to greatness. I am called to be a great dad— the best I can for the two girls who are entrusted to my care. Besides being a husband and partner, being a dad is the most important role I will ever play, even if I could throw a blazing fastball or establish a new religious community.

Consider these words from fellow dad, Blessed Frédéric Ozanam, founder of the St. Vincent de Paul Society:

> My dear friend, one day you will experience the same emotion after several hours of terrible pains [when] you hear the last cry of the mother and the first cry of the newborn child, then suddenly you see a tiny creature appear, that immortal creature of whom one becomes the guardian. At that moment something terrible and yet supremely sweet occurs in the depths of the soul, not in the metaphorical sense but in a real, physical sense. One feels as if the hand of God is remodeling one inwardly and shaping a new heart within.[1]

This book casts the spotlight on the vocation of fatherhood, recognizing the challenges and countless blessings that it brings. It also attempts to capture the work of our God shaping a new heart, as Ozanam puts it, within this cherished vocation.

These pages invite you to see yourself as who God says you are—a bearer of God's divine image. When you see God in yourself and in other people, life's colors are brighter, each moment is precious, and relationships are filled with awe. Every struggle is a teachable experience, and every joy fills your soul. I pray these chapters not only affirm your fatherhood vocation, but they help you come to truly believe these words attributed to St. Catherine of Genoa: "My deepest me is God."

There are many moments when I look at my children and I wonder: If I—and all called to this vocation throughout the generations—truly understood the magnitude of the task, would I still say yes? I am not saying that we ever question its worth or value. Rather, can we fully comprehend the miracle entrusted to us and the responsibility that soon follows? While the conception and birth of a child are their own miracles, the transformation of a father deserves its own special recognition. It is only by God's grace that at times we manage and other times we thrive. Amid it all, if we can take a step back and simply look at the role the God within is calling us to, we would stand in frightful awe.

This book is as much a celebration of fatherhood as it is a source of inspiration. I am inviting you to pause and take that step back to better appreciate the miraculous—not just in your child, but in how the God who dwells in your heart is transforming you in God's very image.

I write this book for the dad-to-be, the dad for many years, or those entrusted as a guardian and someone of influence. I pray these pages serve as inspiration. For some, these pages will preview your own story, one yet to be or currently being written. For others, it will remind you of days gone by, the love you gave, and the lives you nurtured into being.

I write this book for those discerning all their vocations. I pray these pages tug at your heart as you examine your roles, current and future, recognizing how God is speaking to you and through you. Parenthood goes beyond the dyads of father and mother; we are all called to bring life into this world by putting to use the varying gifts and talents we possess. While most of the language in this book centers on fatherhood, please interchange it freely with your current identity, or your vocations in service of others. This book is not meant to be exclusively for fathers. Although it does focus on fatherhood, I pray it can help you reflect on and consider who God is calling you to be in our world.

These pages are reflections from my perspective. While there are many commonalities in this vocation, I bring all of myself, the good and the work in progress. I bring certain privileges, cultural norms, and a contemplative spirituality that shapes my experiences and my approach as a father and as a writer. I am sensitive that there is no one-size-fits-all approach; rather, we as fathers are as diverse as we are complicated. However, we find solidarity in the love of our children and the sacredness in our responsibility.

If you were chosen to raise children, in whatever role God has called you to, I pray these pages illuminate your own vocation and impact.

I write this book for those who may be years away from fatherhood yet sense a deeper calling to this role one day. I pray this book grounds you on your journey through the inevitably bumpy roads that will lead you home. When I was younger, although I was decades away from meeting my wife and eventually, having children, I felt a deep calling to fatherhood. Only as I look in the rearview mirror of my life does it all make sense.

I write this book for the unexpected dad—the one who never anticipated this calling. I pray that, like St. Joseph, you find comfort and courage in this very special role that God has entrusted into your hands and heart.

I write this book for the dad-to-be who feels more pressure, more doubt, more anxiety than he ever imagined, for the husband who is trying to make things better for his beloved partner and their child growing within her.

I write this book for the new dad who is suddenly entrusted with a precious child. On September 27, 2016, in the NICU, our firstborn, Shea, grabbed my finger for the first time. Everything changed. Ozanam's words rang as true as any ever written.

I write this book for the dad who is exhausted from sleepless nights, never-ending diapers, google searches for every bump and fever, and every other lesson to be learned by experience.

I write this book for the man who loses a child. At our first prenatal visit for my wife's second pregnancy, the doctor shared that there was no heartbeat. I grasped for anything or anyone that would help me make sense of the unexpected. If you too have experienced a miscarriage, a stillborn child, or any loss of a child, I pray these words provide the same solidarity and compassion I desperately needed so my broken heart could slowly and quietly heal.

I write this book for the father dropping off his child at daycare or school for the first time, watching his kid grow up faster than he can process, and I write this book for the dad who tries to keep it together through the storms of life. From death, to pandemics, to loss of jobs, to loss of self, I write for you.

I write this book for the dad who extends his phone's data storage so he can keep snapping photos and I write this book for the father who welcomes another child and suddenly falls in love all over again. On May 13, 2020, during a global pandemic, our second born, Lily, entered the world. As I watched her delivery on my phone's FaceTime app, I was lost in this heavenly gift. What a ray of hope during a time of despair.

I write for all who are trying their best, praying that when their children grow up, they see in their old man someone who loved them unconditionally.

Future chapters of my life are yet to be written, when God willing, I watch my children go off to high school and college, enter careers and relationships, and seek answers to the same bigger questions that their dad continues to search for.

These chapters capture the before and the beginning of fatherhood—and perhaps, later, I'll offer a sequel.

Until then, I write for my fellow dads and dads-to-be who yearn to hit the sweet spot on every swing of love. I pray that as fathers we support one another like a team of champions. We may never meet, but we can unite spiritually under the leadership of the one Father we all share as we raise a new generation in love.

It's not likely that our names will echo in the hallowed halls of Cooperstown or be captured in the Vatican's statues or art, but we can hope and pray together that they echo in the hearts of our children.

On our baseball cards, may the stats document the number of our hugs, bedtime kisses, and prayers before meals. May they picture us and our children basking in God's divine love.

I pray my story comforts and inspires, and that together we can celebrate this vocation and support each other in the most important position we will ever play.

1st Inning

# First Pitch

"God gave me an ability to throw a baseball. He chose me for a reason, and I want to honor Him with that."[2]

—Clayton Kershaw

"No vocation is born of itself or lives for itself. A vocation flows from the heart of God and blossoms in the good soil of faithful people. Did not Jesus say: "By this all men will know that you are my disciples, if you have love for one another." (Jn 13:35)[3]

—Pope Francis

Although baseball is not a religion, it can serve as a gateway to a divine encounter and even be a spiritual teacher.

Baseball, like religion, presents rituals and rules, curses and blessings. We collect relics, recount stories, and find comfort and hope in the extraordinary saints and athletes who walked before and among us. Like a religious tradition, loyalty to a specific franchise is passed down from generation to generation and the game is played in beautiful cathedrals, where neighbors and strangers unite.

Walk into Fenway Park or Wrigley Field and you find yourself enriched by a century of memories made by players and fans. When I saw a game in Fenway a few years ago, I walked back into time, thinking of the great Ted Williams hitting .406 in the Red Sox' 1941 campaign and the decades of great players, battling a curse, who called this cherished sandlot home. When I caught a Cubbies game at Wrigley in 2019, I imagined "Mr. Cub" Ernie Banks rounding the bases or the "Sultan of Swat," Babe Ruth, calling his home run shot in the 1932 Fall Classic. Even to a New Yorker the friendly confines felt like home. Shea Stadium was my sacred site. There I learned the game and gathered with loved ones, especially my dad who over the years spent a small fortune for us to watch some wins and many crushing losses from the loge section down the third baseline. There were many Sundays when I said more prayers during the 1:00 p.m. game than I did less than three hours earlier at the 10:30 a.m. Mass.

Baseball invites us to slow down. The only major sport without a clock, the game teaches us to stop and breathe. You are invited to "take" in a game, accepting the space to soak in the sun, and to be lost in the plays and sounds.

This beloved game encompasses three seasons, from hope in spring to acceptance in the fall. The changing weather serves as an appropriate backdrop of the 162-game season, fitting for the always-evolving journey of life.

Faith also grounds the game. It was faith that gave Jackie Robinson the courage to break the color barrier in 1947, and faith that gave Brooklyn Dodgers' executive

Branch Rickey the courage to desegregate the game. He said, "Someday I'm going to have to stand before God, and if He asks me why I didn't let that (Jackie) Robinson fellow play ball, I don't think saying 'because of the color of his skin' would be a good enough answer."[4] Robinson, who faced threats and harassment to play professionally, relied on God to change the game and society. Like Rickey, Robinson was a Methodist, and each night before bed he would fall to his knees to pray. "It's the best way to get closer to God," he said. Six years after Robinson played his first game for the Dodgers, fellow Brooklyn star Gil Hodges found himself in a painful slump, hitting .193 after the first twenty-eight games. It didn't help that he had gone hitless in his last eleven games the year before, including a losing effort in a seven game World Series against the Yankees. As the story goes, Fr. Herbert Rodmond of Brooklyn's St. Francis Roman Catholic Church offered this brief Sunday homily in 1953: "It's far too hot for a homily. Keep the Commandments and say a prayer for Gil Hodges."[5] The prayers of the faithful worked, as Hodges soon found his swing and by the end of the season raised his average to .302. His good fortunes continued, including giving Brooklyn their first and only title two years later. And fourteen years after that, Hodges would manage the "Miracle Mets" to their first championship in 1969.

Watch any game, and you will see a player point to the sky after a big hit or make the sign of the cross before taking his swings. Even Ruth, "the Great Bambino," wore a Miraculous Medal in his final years for comfort and hope. Before undergoing a serious operation, Ruth received the medal from a seventh-grade boy from New Jersey.

Comedian George Carlin famously said in comparing baseball and football: "In baseball the object is to go home! And to be safe! I hope I'll be safe at home." God invites you home, right now, to dwell in divine love. Like Robinson stealing home against the New York Yankees in Game 1 of the 1955 World Series, you too will feel safe and at home when you return to God. The vocation of fatherhood presents that safe pathway home, by discovering God in the mother of your children, in the eyes of your kids, and dwelling within your own championship heart.

### Put Me in Coach

I love being a dad.

Even from a young age, I had a deep sense that I was made to raise children. Although I spent years wondering what to do with my life, I always understood my vocation to fatherhood as a specific call from God. In his book, *Let Your Life Speak*, author and teacher Parker Palmer writes, "Vocation does not mean a goal that I pursue. It means a calling that I hear. Before I can tell my life what I want to do with it, I must listen to my life telling me who I am."[6]

Oddly, long before I met my wife, as my life began to reveal itself, there were moments when this vocation was reinforced. For example, in college I started volunteering at a children's hospital. This turned into a summer job for two consecutive years, often working with children who were very sick. For some, their parents were present, while for others their only parental figures were the heroic nurses and staff that cared for them.

This work was difficult, at times heartbreaking. Yet in the encounters with these children, from playing games to assisting the nurses, my vocation of fatherhood was slowly revealing itself. There were little ones with whom I watched cartoons and one special teenager who several times a week beat me in video games. Many would join me in arts and crafts, and with others I simply sat in silence. In each of these moments, I felt called to be a friend to these children who were battling significant illnesses.

During one Christmas season, I was saddened that some children would be alone. Many families, if their children were well enough, could bring them home for the holiday so they could have a familiar Christmas. For others, families came to them.

One young toddler was well enough to go home, but he didn't have one. When his health improved, he would be adopted or enter the foster system. I knew this particular child, especially since I took him and a few others to Shea Stadium one Saturday afternoon to meet the beloved mascot Mr. Met, take photos in the dugout, and to see a major league ballpark. I am not sure who was more excited, him or me. When that Christmas arrived, I empathized with him, feeling the loneliness and the sadness that the holiday would be no different than any other day. In fact it was worse, since the staff was limited and many other children were absent. I had to do something, so I thought that I could make it brighter by bringing Christmas to him. A few days prior I had bought a four-foot blowup Spiderman toy and on Christmas morning brought it to him.

I remember thinking how this was just a small gesture to lift his spirits, knowing there were structural and personal injustices and circumstances that didn't change his reality. In leaving his room that day to return to my family celebration, it felt like it wasn't enough. . . because it wasn't.

Looking back to those days, I recognize how God was preparing me not only to be a father to my own biological children, but to respond to the needs of others who are alone, struggling, and in need of hope and joy. In all our experiences, God is preparing us for our future encounters, inviting us to answer prayers and transform lives. Every moment is a teachable moment.

At times I think of that young child, who now must be in his early 20s. I ponder how without recognizing him I might pass him in a store or on the road. As I consider this, I understand better our connectedness. Two decades before, we had an impact on one another. Through the passage of distance and time, we would no longer even recognize one another, and it is likely he wouldn't even remember that Christmas morning or any of my other visits. I trust he was formed by it, as I certainly was shaped by his contagious smile and energy.

As we pursue our different vocations, we must remember our connectedness. Consider all your coaches and teachers, everyone who offered a helping hand or a shoulder to cry on. Many you remember, many you do not. You have been formed by the named as well as by those lost from memory. God calls us into a variety of vocations which invite us to utilize our gifts and talents. We often identify with what we do for work, or our major in college, or how we speak, talk, or look. When we move past the exterior, we find the divine. If we truly listen, we discover God's love that drives us into service of others. Once we know God's love, we can't help but to share it with all we encounter.

Is this not what parents do?

This new creation is entrusted to you, and your life is no longer about you alone, or about you and your partner. It is now about your child. God is a God of surprises, a God who answers prayers. This deeper calling literally changes the world.

Frederick Buechner famously wrote, "The place God calls you to is the place where your deep gladness and the world's deep hunger meet."[7] If you approach fatherhood from this mindset, you understand better the greater impact of this vocation.

## Most Valuable Dad

In the Christian tradition, when we think of fathers, our attention often goes to St. Joseph, the earthly father of Jesus. For two thousand years, we have applauded this carpenter for his faithfulness to Mary, his raising of Jesus, and his heroic behavior in the Nativity story. In the Christian scriptures Joseph does not utter a single word, yet his limited actions and love of God echo through time, drawing our attention and praise. In Jesus we see the impact of Joseph's primary vocation. The disciples call Jesus "Rabbi," because he is a great teacher of the law. Who taught Jesus such things? While we gain glimpses of the divine, especially when Jesus is preaching in the temple at a young age, we must give some, if not much, credit to Joseph and Mary.

Joseph raised his son under a cloud of misunderstanding and doubt. Imagine the whispers that must have followed the Holy Family. Picture the gossip outside the temple, and the questions amid the unknown. Joseph's care for Mary when she is with child is legendary. Scripture tells us that he wished to divorce Mary quietly to save her from "public disgrace" (Mt 1:18). But then, in a dream, an angel tells Joseph, "Do not be afraid" (Mt 1:20). He is instructed to take Mary as his wife, and the angel explains that Mary had conceived by the Holy Spirit and will give birth to Jesus (Mt 1:20-21).

I am grateful when I encounter the words in scripture, "Be not afraid." This humanizes the characters, reminding us that they are more than historical figures—they are real people, like us, filled with questions, emotions, and complexities. Joseph was afraid, as any new parent can relate. In all that Joseph hears from the angel, what is really being said is "trust God." And Joseph does—and the world rejoices.

The familiar Christmas hymn, "O Holy Night" contains that beautiful line, "Til He [Jesus] appears, and the soul felt its worth." When we recognize God, be it in the baby Jesus, your small or big child, or anyone entrusted to our care, our souls feel their worth. It is why we were created. It is our calling.

Some of you may have a story familiar to mine. I married my best friend, and we were blessed with biological children. Many others may have a different journey to fatherhood. You may be raising children as a single father, in a union with another father, as a stepfather, uncle, grandfather, separated from the mother, or you may be blessed by adoption. As I wrote earlier, fatherhood takes many forms. My experiences may reflect the most familiar depiction of this vocation, but by looking at St. Joseph we see one of the greatest fatherly examples and his nontraditional relationship with his Mary and his Jesus.

## Playing for Others

The vocation of fatherhood presents a challenge for those who have had a rocky or painful relationship with their own father or other father figures. The call to this vocation can open past wounds, presenting varying emotions. I think of what Henri Nouwen wrote: "In a world so torn apart by rivalry, anger, and hatred, we have the privileged vocation to be living signs of a love that can bridge all division and heal all wounds."[8] God makes all things new. In this vocation of fatherhood, you are a living sign of love, bridging internal and external division, and healing wounds—including your own.

This requires greater support and community centered around God. Grounded in faith and trust, it's better for fathers to support one another instead of going at it alone. The Western culture's expectation for individual responsibility and success is unrealistic and, honestly, unfair. Jesus, as he began his ministry, brought people together. It was the first Christian community where they learned, served, and loved.

Imagine a space where fathers can just be together, not to compete or to compare, not to judge or to limit.

Envision a common bond that can, if supported, draw out the best in all of us. For several years, I led a youth ministry at St. Mel's Parish in Queens, New York. It was a blessed time for us—my wife and I, and a group of friends who shared a commitment to the youth of the parish. The fathers too shared that commitment. It was impressive to see this group of dads from the parish come together at different points of the year to create a space for their children. I recall my father and others doing the same when I was young at our home parish, Nativity of the Blessed Virgin Mary, also in Queens. Most notably, starting several weeks before Halloween, the fathers at St. Mel's would come by after work and build, transforming an empty hall into a "haunted house." Several weeks later they would transform the room again, this time, creating a Christmas village and train show. These same men coached the CYO athletic teams, worshiped with their families on Sunday, and managed all personal and professional responsibilities.

While this community's shared projects are a gift to all involved, we need more and more to celebrate fathers beyond what they do and to create a space where fathers can speak openly and honestly about this sacred vocation.

As you journey through this book and explore your personal vocation, be open and creative to how you will create a space for you and for your fellow fathers to unite, to grow, and to support one another.

In their book, *From Wild Man to Wise Man: Reflections on Male Spirituality*, Richard Rohr and Joseph Martos offer this important insight on spirituality from the male perspective:

A masculine spirituality would be one that encourages men to take the radical gospel journey from their own unique beginning point, in their own unique style, with their own unique goals. . . . That takes immense courage and self-possession. Such a man has life for others and knows it. He does not need to push, intimidate or play the power games common to other men because he possesses his power with surety and self-confidence.[9]

What a mission statement for fatherhood! I am drawn most to the notion of "a life for others and knows it." This is a vocation of service, of love.

Throughout these pages, focus your attention on the goodness, the kindness, and the inspirational opportunities and possibilities of this vocation. Discover the unique call of fatherhood, owning it as perhaps the greatest of your responsibilities. Increase your trust that the God who dwells within is leading you into the Father's Hall of Fame. In return, reveal the faith that God shows in you to your children.

In his remarks at his induction into Major League Baseball's Hall of Fame in 2016, former New York Mets all-star catcher, Mike Piazza, said this of his father: "My father's faith in me, often greater than my own, is the single most important factor of me being inducted into this Hall of Fame. Thank you, Dad."[10] The faith that fathers have in their children is the cornerstone of their own journey. The faith they provide, and the faith in God that they teach and model, grounds their children to seek and attain their own vocations and peace.

In 2021, on Good Shepherd Sunday, Pope Francis tweeted: "St. Joseph is an outstanding example of accepting God's plans. May he help everyone, especially those who are discerning, to make God's dreams for them come true. May he grant them the courage to say "yes" to the Lord who always surprises and never disappoints."[11]

Saying "yes" to a vocation, be it fatherhood, motherhood, married life, priesthood, religious life, single life, is a response to God's calling. God planted this call in your heart for you to accept and to act upon. As 2016 World Series MVP, Ben Zobrist said, "I don't have anything to boast about—there is nothing I can say I've done. I can say my biggest success is Christ did things through me."[12]

At the beginning of this chapter, we sought inspiration from St. Joseph, reminded of his special and critical role in the life of his holy family and yours. In the next chapter, we will imagine the support Joseph found in his beloved Mary and in others, all leading to your own examination of where you find a similar community and solidarity.

# Teammates

"The way a team plays as a whole determines its success. You may have the greatest bunch of individual stars in the world, but if they don't play together, the club won't be worth a dime."[13]

—Babe Ruth

"The only answer in this life, to the loneliness we are all bound to feel, is community. The living together, working together, sharing together, loving God and loving our brother, and living close to him in community so we can show our love for Him."[14]

—Dorothy Day

Fatherhood, like baseball, is not a game played alone. Unlike basketball, where one player can dominate the game, baseball requires a team effort. Even if your pitcher is throwing a perfect game, you still need your offense to score (unless you're Catfish Hunter, who in 1968 was responsible for three of the four runs that his Oakland A's scored as he pitched a perfect game).[15]

For many, a father's closest teammate is his spouse, the one who takes the physical brunt of the work during pregnancy, delivery, and in those opening months where even as she recovers she still takes care of (and in many cases nurses) their newborn. Of all my baseball heroes, not one ever inspired me as my wife, Suzie, did and does in raising our children. She has played some amazing innings.

In May of 2020 she played the most challenging inning so far when, during a global pandemic, she gave birth to our second daughter, Lily. I could not be at her side as I stayed home with Shea. Wearing an n95 mask for three days straight, Suzie gave birth by a C-section surgical delivery. She guarded Lily, never letting our child leave her sight. When I picked her up from the hospital, she gingerly walked to the car. Lily was so small that at first I couldn't even notice that Suzie was holding her close to her chest. That journey home was Suzie's tired home run trot.

Suzie's other great inning was giving birth to our first daughter, Shea. After four days of labor and a difficult delivery, it took over ten hours to regain enough strength and clarity to stand from her bed. During that time, Shea was in the NICU under observation for pneumonia and other complications. Suzie's heroic struggle to walk the nearly one hundred yards to the NICU, six times a day for three days, revealed her greatness. With the care of some skilled and caring nurses she slowly recovered, as did Shea, and every day since I have seen her live out her vocation.

This is my story. You have your own (or one day you will!).

For some fathers, the mother of your children may not be, or may no longer be, your wife. For others, the mother may be a distant brave woman who entrusted her child to your care. Your teammate(s) in raising children may include your spouse or partner, your parents, other family members, and friends. Together, you can become a team who step up to the plate whenever you are called.

## Team Win

You have heard it said over and over: "It takes a village." I cannot tell you how often these words echo through my grateful heart as I watch my daughters grow. Think of all the nurses, doctors, teachers, spiritual leaders, family members, and friends who support you and your children in this vocation. Recall those who dropped off food, said a prayer, sent gifts or a message or a card of love. Remember those who listened when your tank was empty and those who reminded you of God's presence in your child's creation story. As I said, it's a team game.

The greatest game I witnessed in person was at Shea Stadium—Game Five of the 1999 National League Championship Series between the Atlanta Braves and the Mets. If they beat my beloved Mets, the Braves would head to the World Series. The game lasted fifteen innings, a then-postseason record five hours and forty-six minutes. In the final minute, Mets third baseman Robin Ventura hit the infamous "Grand Slam Single" to win the game and send the series back to Atlanta (his teammates mobbed Ventura before he could get even to second base, so only one of four potential runs counted—but it was enough). Besides Ventura's walk-off home run, the most important hit of that game came from pinch-hitter Shawon Dunston. To start the bottom of the fifteenth inning, with the Mets down a run, Dunston, in a nine-minute at bat, worked the count to three balls and two strikes. He proceeded to foul off six consecutive pitches before hitting a single up the middle to set the table for the miraculous comeback. That day began with nine players from each side on the field; before it was over forty-five had taken part, twenty-three of them for the victorious Mets. It indeed takes a village.

In our lives, and with this vocation, it takes a team to raise a family. I could write this whole book just about teammates who, like Dunston, came through and have let me be the best father I can be to my children. When I walk through the door I may get the hero's welcome from my young daughters, but I am only one of the many who send love and support and show up to strengthen and protect my family.

## Hello Joe, Again

In the previous chapter, we turned to St. Joseph and as noted earlier, the accounts of Joseph are limited. We often consider Joseph's protection of Mary after she reveals her pregnancy and in their journey to Nazareth, but we may not recall Mary's protection of Joseph.

We will never know their nighttime chats, their long walks, and their warm embraces, but we trust that they supported one another. Looking at the fruit they produced, we see how they created a home for Jesus, a divine king. If we allow our imaginations to complete the full picture, we could envision Joseph sharing his anxiety and fears with his wife. We can see him coming home from work with his tired and sore hands from toiling at carpentry and masonry. We can picture Mary tending his wounds, both inside and out.

When Jesus disappears as an adolescent, you may relate to the worry that both Mary and Joseph felt. Imagine that night as a relieved Joseph recovers and ponders how his son could teach with such wisdom at the temple. Imagine Mary reminding Joseph of the presence of God in their lives and in their son, preparing their hearts for what was to come.

We do not know when Joseph died, but scriptural historians assume it came before Jesus' crucifixion, since he is not mentioned as being present on Golgotha. We can try to imagine Joseph's final day: Jesus would be there, as would Mary—the Holy Family united one last time in this world. Perhaps Joseph died before Jesus started his ministry, or Jesus may have returned from his travels to mourn his father as he did for his cousin Lazarus. You can picture the scene: Joseph, resting and preparing for his last breath. Mary and Jesus praying, offering words of gratitude and love. From Joseph's perspective, he would see his heroic spouse, humanity's God-bearer. Joseph would see his son, humanity's Savior. Would he, did he, fully appreciate the role he played in this greatest story in human history?

We do not have to wait until our deathbed to appreciate the divine in our midst. We can look into the eyes of our many teammates and see how God's holy hand moves through them. We can look at our children and wonder at their existence and at their beauty. If we look back over all the innings that have come before, we might be overwhelmed with gratitude for how God used others to bring us to this point in our life.

## Filling Out Your Lineup Card

In contrast to the enormous pressure that Western society places on individuals to achieve and to succeed, the vocation of fatherhood requires community. Looking back at my own life I wonder how much easier it could have been, how healthier I could have felt, if I allowed others to walk with me.

I invite my first-year students at the university to participate in an explorative activity where they identify their own personal Board of Trustees. I give them a worksheet with the diagram of a long oval table with space for eight to ten seats. They are to name "chairs" for different aspects of their life. For example, who would they choose for advice about handling money, about their major and career choices, about their spiritual life and about relationships. Like my students, we ultimately are responsible for making our own decisions, but these wisdom figures play an important role—if we let them.

As fathers, it is useful to name not just wisdom figures, but those who can listen, offering perspective and support. A father's Board of Trustees might include someone you call for car or house trouble, a mental health counselor, a spiritual director, a parenting advisor, a coach for navigating school and sports teams, a

financial planner, a fellow father for solidarity, and—
above all—a partner who shares the same hopes and
goals for your child or children.

While this activity helps provide direction and can
even prioritize responsibilities, it also reveals your team.
Like the image of your starting lineup on a score card,
you clearly see who is on your side, working toward the
same goal, and ready to share their unique gifts with
you and your family.

There is a Native American (Sioux) proverb, "With
all things and in all things, we are relatives." Once we
understand and appreciate the relatives we have, blood-
related and not, we can better fulfill this vocation. We
see the necessity of such relatives in our generations of
tired, often angry and wounded fathers. They carry the
burdens of their world as crosses, until they fall.

But in every life there are many Simon of Cyrenes
to help carry the crosses, and in some cases, even to
remove the burden. The vocation of fatherhood is
not meant to drain you or to kill you—in fact, it is the
opposite. If we allow others to help us carry our crosses
and to support us, the vocation can be joyful, filled with
energy, gratitude, and appreciation.

In filling out your lineup card you can also include
God, to lay the burden down before your Creator. Since
the vocation to fatherhood comes from God, you can
trust that God equips you with what and who you need.
God not only walks beside you but lives within you as
you create and nurture life. As you create and recreate
your home through every fortuitous or unlucky bounce
of the ball, be secure that it is centered on God's love.
Take as your own one of St. Augustine's rules for his

community: "The main reason you are gathered in the same house is to live in harmony and to be united in mind and heart as you strive toward God."[16]

Finally, as we wrap up this inning, take time to recognize the important role you have played in others' lives and are playing right now. The times you show up and respond. The "chairs" you fill in the support network of your "relatives." The crosses you carry to provide relief. You may not realize how often you are the answer to prayer. If you did, perhaps you would better understand this life, your role in it, and the many ways you respond to God's call.

3rd Inning

# The Call

"Today, I consider myself the luckiest man on the face of the earth."[7]

—Lou Gehrig

"The angel of the Lord appeared to him in a dream and said, 'Joseph, son of David, do not be afraid.'"

—Matthew 1:20

Most of us will never be summoned into a minor league manager's office to be told that we've been called up to the big leagues. Since the game's humble beginnings in 1876, just over twenty thousand have received that call to "the Show." Many more of us receive a different call—the call to fatherhood. On three different occasions, I received this blessed call from my wife.

The first occurred on January 25, 2016. It was a "snow day" from work, as well as the Foundation Day of the Vincentian community. I am a four-time graduate of St. John's University, and I presently serve there as a campus minister and faculty member. The University was founded by the Congregation of the Mission, a religious group of priests that follow the teaching of St. Vincent de Paul. Vincent was a priest in seventeenth century France, who transformed the country by his care and service to the poor. He was the father of a variety of communities committed to this service. It was appropriate that on this special day, Suzie shared a pregnancy test that accounted for her strange feelings over the past few weeks. When you find out that you will be a father, you can't predict how you will feel. For myself, as much as I always wanted to hear those words, my initial response was not positive. I first felt shock. We were open and hoping for children, but that day I was not expecting to receive this news. Walking to the store later that morning, I kept asking myself if this was really happening.

This saying is attributed to St. Vincent de Paul: "All beginnings are somewhat strange; but we must have patience, and little by little, we shall find things, which at first were obscure, becoming clearer." It was strange indeed! Instead of being full of excitement, I was full of worry: did we have enough money, was our apartment big enough, would Suzie and my baby be healthy, were we ready? Only through prayer and time did the shock and worry fade into heavenly joy.

One such joy was telling family and friends. My favorite memory was meeting my parents for dinner to break the news. They were so excited that they wanted to tell everyone in the restaurant. It was wonderful to share this news of new life with so many who cared for us deeply.

When we found out, we were in a place of stability. Not everyone has this benefit. Depending on your circumstances, at first you might not welcome the conception of your child. However, God's grace always enters and then, and only then, you can move from a place of fear to a place of jubilant acceptance. As the angel said to Mary and Joseph, "Be not afraid!"

Soon the doctor visits began, and they were both monumental and frightening. I recall going back to that small room and hearing the heartbeat for the first time. Despite my fear of bad news, I celebrated as from visit to visit I watched our daughter grow. We marked every good news visit, often with omelets and coffee at the local diner.

As the pregnancy progressed, we both looked forward to finding out the gender. Suzie received the doctor's call one day when we were both at work, and then later, over dinner at our favorite restaurant, she handed me a small card with two onesies revealing that we were having a girl. Now we could focus our excitement on narrowing down potential names. And then, at 12:59 p.m. on September 27—the feast day of St. Vincent—our daughter Shea was born. In chapter 5 I'll recount the experience of that day.

Several years after Shea's birth, Suzie wasn't feeling well and suspected she might be pregnant. The month before her first doctor's visit was filled with anticipation and excitement, especially as it coincided with Christmas. As the calendar turned, however, so did our lives. We did not leave that first doctor's visit holding a sonogram. Instead, we could only clutch one another as tears of despair fell. In chapter 6, I will share this difficult experience in more detail.

Over ten months after this second pregnancy, Suzie met me after work for a happy hour. When the waiter arrived to take our order, Suzie requested only water. I first supposed she wanted to eat something before ordering a cocktail, but she soon revealed that she was not drinking because once again we had been blessed.

Cautious from our experience with the previous pregnancy, we tiptoed through the opening weeks. When we entered the doctor's office for the first visit, I was prepared for the worst. As the doctor calmly searched for the heartbeat, every second in that sterile room was excruciating. Unsure of what the sonogram was revealing, I anxiously waited for the sound of a beating heart. Soon enough, the doctor said, "All looks good," then we heard the baby's heartbeat. We left this office with a refrained excitement. We knew what could happen and until we made it to the three-month mark, our little girl remained our special secret.

These are precious moments from my life, and the creation stories of my children and my path as a father. You may resonate with these experiences, or your journey might be very different. What unites us in this life-changing scenario is the closing of one chapter and the beginning of another. We are bonded by the active role we play in creating life through the love of God.

## Becoming an Ace

Throughout our lives God presents moments of transformation, perhaps none bigger than creating and nurturing new life. Often enough, a multitude of "little deaths" make way for our resurrections. Those little deaths slowly, and at times painfully, carve and shape you for the future. You journey toward this most heroic of vocations by way of broken roads, broken hearts, and broken dreams. Only by looking into the past with a grateful heart can you appreciate what was and discover grace for where you are now.

As you prepare for new life, your priorities begin to shift and the little deaths come one after another. You dig deeper into your soul, finding that while God is creating new life in the mother's womb, God is also creating a new you.

Photos from the B.C. (Before Children) period of our lives reveal less grey hair and fewer wrinkles. Along with these bodily changes, my perspective has changed too, and this blessed experience has made my relationship with God deeper and richer.

Perhaps the greatest spiritual challenge of fatherhood is being able to trust while remaining present to the blessings before you. Living like this echoes the familiar psalm, "Be still and know that I am God" (Ps 46:10). This became my mantra, from every doctor visit to the herculean task of putting together a crib and dresser for the baby's room.

A deeper relationship with God allows you to be quiet amid endless noise. This sacred encounter makes you recognize how you are already united with God and with others. Often, we focus our lives on personal gain and success. Fatherhood invites you to see life as greater than your own individual narrative. Letting go of the story of you and seeing your life as an indwelling for the divine lets you release your stress, fear, and anxiety. God invites you into something greater and deeper.

In the later years of his life, as the focus of his prayer shifted from concern with "I" to the "One" to whom he prayed, the twentieth century mystic, Thomas Merton wrote these words:"[18]

> Oh, God, we are one with You. You have made us one with You. You have taught us that if we are open to one another, You dwell in us. Help us to preserve this openness and to fight for it with all our hearts. Help us to realize that there can be no understanding where there is mutual rejection. Oh God, in accepting one another wholeheartedly, fully, completely, we accept You, and we thank You, and we adore You, and we love You with our whole being, because our being is in Your being, our spirit is rooted in Your spirit. Fill us then with love, and let us be bound together with love as we go our diverse ways, united in this one spirit which makes You present in the world, and which makes You witness to the ultimate reality that is love. Love has overcome. Love is victorious. Amen.[19]

In any relationship, you cannot trust someone that you do not know. Pregnancy—like every stage of life— invites you to invest time with your Creator. During this precious time, you are invited to remain present to what Eckhart Tolle calls "the Now." "Surrender to what it is," Tolle writes. "Say 'yes' to life."[20]

After what will feel like the blink of an eye, your baby will emerge from the womb. Cherish this time, as it is never guaranteed and may never occur again. This is the same after your child is born and begins to grow. Look up from your phone, put away your computer, set aside the endless to-do list and simply be present to the miracles that surround you.

During the 1980 All-Star game at Dodger Stadium, hall of fame announcer Vin Scully noted, "It's a mere moment in a man's life between an All-Star game and an old-timers game." When I found out we were having our first baby, I feared that we weren't ready. I was caught up with the size of our apartment and bank account. But God was shaping what was most important—my heart. I was ready to give that heart to my child, and children, hopefully revealing God's love to them each day.

Crucial to the spiritual life is a grateful heart—grateful for what was, for what will be, and for what is. A grateful heart lets you learn from the unexpected and the unwanted. It lets you be fully present. I do not prefer waking up at two in the morning to change a diaper, but it only takes a second for my heart to become grateful. As my gaze is drawn into my daughter's tired blue eyes, I forget my fatigue and am once again wrapped around her finger. All I see is this divine gift, this miraculous light.

In all its forms, life is a miracle. At conception we find a flicker of the divine. In 2016, researchers discovered that when an ovum is fertilized, the rapid release of zinc creates a "microscopic flash of light."[21] Science does not contradict but confirms spirituality and religion. The moment of fertilization, a moment of light, reminds us of the divine intelligence that created all things. Jesus said "You are the light of the world" (Mt 5:18). Light is who you are, and if you pay attention you can see it. Look into the eyes of children, a pregnant mother, a new dad. Look into the eyes of grandparents holding their offspring's offspring, of a family reunited after some separation, of someone nearing the end of their earthly journey. From beginning to end we are light.

A number of years ago, one of my favorite uncles passed away. I share more of this story in chapter 6. During our final conversation, as we were speaking to each other about the love of God, his tired eyes revealed that divine light. More than ninety years before that moment his mother and father conceived him. That divine spark didn't flicker out when he took his last breath. Instead, it returned to where it came from. God creates new life through our active participation, and he has us play perhaps our greatest role in allowing divine light to shine in our children.

When a man finds out he is becoming a father, he cannot help but wonder who his child will be, what that child will look like, how that baby will transform the world for the better. Over the next nine months he and his spouse ride a roller coaster experience of doctor visits, cravings, health concerns, added responsibilities, the building of furniture, and a transformation of not only the baby room, but the inner workings of the soul.

Like a championship season that begins with hope in April, the nine-month journey toward October glory is a cherished time that lives in your heart forever.

# Spring Training

"Baseball is like driving, it's the one who gets home safely that counts."[22]

—Tommy Lasorda

"Do everything in love."

—1 Cor 16:14

As your child grows in the mother's womb, life changes quickly. For some fortunate women, at its worst pregnancy brings strange cravings and sore feet. Many others experience an array of symptoms, presenting new challenges that summon the father and loved ones to assume greater responsibilities.

During her first pregnancy, Suzie was very ill and in the final months, a few laps around St. John's University's Carnesecca Arena was a stretch. When she was pregnant with Lily, she battled two separate hospitalizations, a pandemic, and an unexpected change of home. Talk about an MVP season. Through it all, I tried to take on more and more roles to alleviate her pain and not to add additional stress to her life.

Attention is directed to the mother and the baby growing within her, and rightly so, but the father is going through his own transformation. Much like spring training, it is a time of preparation, conditioning, practice, and anticipation.

As the due date approaches the season takes on more and more stress. Dads-to-be may begin to look inward, questioning if they are ready for this responsibility. Some wounds are re-opened, while positive and negative emotional and mental thoughts grow in intensity and volume. If a father can be reflective and seek support, this can be a time of transformation and growth. If it is ignored or buried inside, the process can become more frustrating, and he may find himself in an extended slump.

When the COVID-19 pandemic struck our world in 2020, I was faced with a different moment of growth. I not only feared Lily's delivery that spring when my hometown Queens was rattled as the world's epicenter of the coronavirus, I also faced my own mortality and what that meant for my loved ones. And for me.

## Night Game

Like never before I feared death. Each night I struggled as ambulance lights strobed through my bedroom window. Instead of counting sheep, I imagined my family without me. I wondered if my oldest would even remember me. I feared what the loss of love and income would mean for my wife and children, how my parents would survive it, and how my loved ones and friends would suffer in sadness.

I feared my own destiny. What would happen to me? Where would I go? What is heaven like, if I am invited? Would I see loved ones? And if I did, would I even recognize them? Would they know me? What if all that I was taught had been only an elaborate coping strategy to survive this crazy world with a somewhat sane mind. I struggled with these fearful questions as I spent too many dark nights to count lacking the trust and faith that I once took for granted.

In time, I recognized my life was shifting, and in the depth of this darkness, a deeper, more significant relationship with God was starting to flourish. As songwriter and poet Leonard Cohen wrote, "There is a crack in everything. That's how the light gets in." My prayer turned into a wrestling match between faith and lack of trust. When my faith was absent and I couldn't fully trust that God indeed was my loving creator, I found glimpses of hope in the words of spiritual leaders, such as Chiara Lubich. Lubich writes, "If the mercy of God grants this, death will mean seeing Mary, seeing Jesus. How then can we surround that passage with mourning, even . . . if it comes with the harsh reality of an agony, be it long or short, and in any case with the breakdown of the human shells of our lives?"[23]

Lubich, the founder of the Focolare Movement, faced great suffering in her life. Bombs literally fell over her head when her hometown Trent was under attack in World War II. She emerged from a time of great disruption, pain, and loss with a deeper relationship with God and trust in him. Lubich was able to do this because she belonged to a community grounded in prayer, scripture, and service, that lived in unity and grew together in relationship with God.

Lady Julian of Norwich writes:
Know it well, love is its meaning.

Who reveals this to you? Love.
What does he reveal? Love. Why? For Love.
Remain in this and you will know more of the same.²⁴

Growing in relationship with God invited me to glimpse the mystery that God is love, and from this source comes all things. Learning to embrace this love, to really believe it, remains the greatest of in-game challenges. To help myself embrace this and believe it, I turned in prayer to loved ones who had passed, those whose lives reflected this love. Among many others I thought of my grandfather, my aunt, my mentor, my friend. I reflected on their love and at times in prayer, I could still feel it.

I recalled those moments in life when I gained glimpses of heaven. There was a time in Assisi, before the remains of St. Francis, when I was overwhelmed with peace and where I claimed my vocation. There was an experience in Lourdes when a long-time volunteer looked into my eyes and taught me to serve the sick who would soon be arriving. There was one night in the Vatican when I felt the energy in the room change simply by being in the presence of St. John Paul II. And there was that day when my fiancée became my wife and the tears and champagne never stopped flowing.

With a grateful heart, I look back at the many moments that have revealed God's loving and guiding hand as I respond to life's nudges and shoves. I see why, in this life and the next, I have every reason to trust God. As poet Ralph Waldo Emerson wrote, "All I have seen teaches me to trust the creator for all I have not seen." At the age of eighty-five, psychologist Florida

Scott-Maxwell wrote these words: "You need only claim the events of your life to make yourself yours. When you truly possess all you have been and done . . . you are fierce with reality."[25] With deeper faith, and greater appreciation for who you are, you will better understand God's love. As I walk this mysterious journey with you, I continue to learn how all my experiences, talents, and especially my suffering, have prepared me for this vocation, and all the positions I play in this game of life.

## Coaching Staff

A few months after Lily was born, I expanded my own community by seeking out experts for guidance and fresh perspective. Like a former slugger looking to reclaim his home run swing, I sought out both a spiritual director and a mental health counselor. My spiritual director welcomed God into the conversation and helped me learn how to connect once more with the divine. I related to St. Francis and St. Ignatius, for whom a time of quarantine and isolation were an invitation for transformation. I shared my frustrations in prayer and fear of the pandemic, and although I stood in the valley of the shadow of death, I soon learned to trust so God could restore my soul (Psalm 23). This remains a familiar spiritual challenge.

My mental health counselor shifted my perspective, helping me look to the past so I could learn new strategies that would bring acceptance and peace. I processed and prayed with some of those internal voices shaped by the said and unsaid. I learned new skills and techniques, all while claiming my identities and voice. Through all of this, I am reminded and invited to trust in the Source who leads me beside still waters (Psalm 23).

It took me a while to come to a place where I was ready to discuss such matters and to be fully capable of listening. It took me even longer to write about it with honesty and authenticity. While I wish I started these healthy processes earlier, on a deeper level, I understand that it was all in God's perfect time. As the saying goes, when the student is ready, the teacher arrives.

As I look back at this painful time, I see that the challenges invited me into a deeper relationship with God. As a result, I am a better husband, father, son, minister, writer, and friend. I continue to work on it like a hitter practicing his swing in the batting cage before the game, trying to improve while remaining exceptionally kind to myself.

"Baseball in general has been a challenge," said former Pittsburg Pirates MVP Andrew McCutchen. "(God) helps in the midst of struggle and what I've been going through. On the field, sometimes, things don't go your way, but through Him, He gets my spirit in the right frame of mind."[26]

I share this as I hope to assist even slightly in removing the stigma of counseling, and discussing emotions and mental health, especially for men. I also stress the importance of spiritual direction. You will benefit from reflecting on how the Holy Spirit is moving in and through you and others. I truly believe we can all flourish with trained experts who can lead us to the best version of ourselves.

From the baseball diamond, I recall the resurgence of World Champion and October hero Justin Verlander.

He was Rookie of the Year in 2006, the Cy Young winner and Most Valuable Player in 2011 but in 2014, at thirty-one years of age, he suffered an injury and could not regain his velocity. Brad Ausmus, his manager with the Detroit Tigers, through analytics taught him how he could regain past success.[27] This new insight transformed Verlander's career and made baseball history. Most notably, in 2017 he led the Houston Astros to their first and only World Series trophy, and in 2019 would win the Cy Young award again. Verlander sought improvement by consulting his coaches and using advancements in technology. How he shifted his life to evolve as a pitcher is an example for our own leadership and life.

Richard Rohr writes, "The word change normally refers to new beginnings. But transformation . . . more often happens not when something new begins but when something old falls apart."[28]

Throughout your life, there will be those bullpen collapses, blowout losses, and season-ending injuries. During unique seasons like a pregnancy, you will wrestle with the past, anxiously await the future, and try to learn from the present. The God who dwells within is guiding you—if you will listen. Allow those angels in disguise in your life to support your transformation and to prepare you to respond to God's call.

### Spiritual Training

This chapter has focused on the transformation of a father-to-be as the baby grows in the mother's womb. Much is written about what a woman might feel each week, how her body and soul is preparing for childbirth. There is an equal amount, if not more, written regarding the baby's daily growth. Each day, something new transforms in this miraculous process.

What is often not discussed is the father's spiritual transformation. You may find some tongue-in-cheek references to how the dad-to-be gains weight as he joins the mother-to-be in satisfying those late-night cravings, but little is written or discussed on how the father is being shaped to welcome his child into this world. I hope you consider this time of preparation as an invitation to enhance your skills. There is much to learn and discover. I remember those first OB-GYN visits and wondering if I should even be there. I would make awkward jokes that missed the mark, often leading to the nurse or doctor rolling their eyes, clearly having heard these one-liners before. As the due date approached, I learned how to paint a dresser and "baby proof" our home. I learned more about diapers, strollers, and car seats than I could have ever imagined.

During my wife's pregnancies I also learned the importance of spiritual work to prepare me for what was to come. As with many other aspects of life, you can try to ignore this spiritual dimension. In some cases it will still sneak up on you, but in others, it will remain tucked away behind the business of the mind and of life. However, if you can better engage with your spiritual self during this pregnancy, and then as a father, you will recognize the ongoing transformation of your heart. As Henri Nouwen writes, "The spiritual life is not a life before, after, or beyond our everyday experience. No, the spiritual life can only be real when it is lived in the midst of the pains and joys of here and now."[29] This spiritual preparation features three key strategies: finding time to pray, seeking inspiration, and staying humble.

## Finding Time to Pray

Finding time to pray is not easy, especially when you are dragging your feet from interrupted sleep and the increasing anxiety of the pregnancy and, eventually, children. Yet, like those many glasses of water needed for our body, prayer nourishes our soul.

Faith communities of worship and prayer bring comfort and solidarity. Whenever we join others in shared prayer, we better fulfill the call to be the body of Christ. Finding ways to pray formal prayers may allow for the familiar words to shape your mind and heart. Sinking into the repetition of praying the rosary or novenas allows for our spirit to be grounded and guided. Prayer need not be limited to structure and rigidness. In your daily actions, from brushing your teeth to cleaning the refrigerator, your awareness to the divine can invite God into these normally mundane experiences.

Since taking on this practice, I am often struck by the blue birds that fly outside my window while I'm preparing breakfast. By simply allowing my mind to be silent and present to God, all encounters have the potential to be miraculous. As Thomas Keating writes, "God is a tremendous supporter of creation, especially all living beings."[30]

During the pandemic, I began practicing meditation for ten minutes per day. It started out as a technique I used while my daughters napped to reduce my anxiety. Over time, I realized how my mind shifted because of this centering exercise. Even when I was not in a meditative state, I felt calm and my thoughts were clearer. I was more grateful and more compassionate. I meditated by centering on the divine light that shines within me. I repeated mantras that grounded my thoughts and my heart. Mantras like "I am love," and "Be still and know that I am God," centered my soul. The more I meditated, I soon found that ten minutes was no longer enough. I started to understand why so many spiritual teachers create time for meditative prayer to begin and end their days.

Although you may want to pray, you may ask yourself, "When do I find the time? This saying is attributed to Martin Luther: "I have so much to do that I shall spend the first three hours in prayer." I would invite you to examine your schedule. Perhaps redirect to prayer those minutes you spend scanning Twitter for sports news, or binge one less episode before you go to sleep. This will soon no longer feel like an uncomfortable chore. Find what works for you and allow your heart and mind to reconnect. Find God there.

"Just be patient and wait," says All-Star shortstop Francisco Lindor. "Keep on believing and keep on praying because it will all be ok. Always find ways to talk to God. It doesn't matter what time of day or night. He will be there. Whenever you can talk to God, it's always special and unique. I love to talk to God. I love to pray."[31]

One final note—What worked in your prayer life at one moment may no longer be fulfilling. We evolve and we transform. Be open to discovering God in all things.

## Seeking Inspiration

The second strategy is to seek inspiration. While every journey is unique, we can learn from those who walked before us. Consult your elders and wisdom figures. Learn from their wisdom, process their advice, and reflect on how God is speaking through them. Read often (especially sacred scripture), watch inspirational videos, and talk with spiritual teachers. Find ways to serve among angels in disguise who reveal not only how to use your time and talents to best advantage, but also to recognize your own blessings.

When Shea was born, a respected father of seven from my home parish shared how at the end of each day, he wrote a note to each of his kids. Sometimes the words were many, other days they were just a thought or a memory from something they might have said or done. On each of his children's wedding days, he handed them a package filled with the countless notes that he crafted through the years. It was a treasure chest of love.

While I could not commit to that task, I found my own way to mark my children's moments. I try to take a photo every day, and in my writing, I attempt to capture the words they say, their own exploration, and their growth. When I published my first book, *Dreams Come True: Discovering God's Vision for Your Life*, I wrote that if only my daughter (I would now add "daughters") read this and felt God's and my love for her, the effort of writing that book was worth it.

I also turn to the saints and other spiritual leaders for their insight. I found great inspiration in the writings of many father figures, especially St. Thomas More, Dr.

Martin Luther King Jr., and Blessed Frédéric Ozanam. I looked to my own father, and to father figures whose actions and words provide a healthy foundation. As a father of two girls, I am especially drawn to my fellow fathers of daughters. I am blessed with friends who teach me how to walk this special path.

## Staying Humble

The third strategy for spiritual preparation is humble action. Hall of Famer Satchel Page is attributed to have said, "You win a few, you lose a few. Some get rained out. But you got to dress for all of them." In other words, being a father means showing up every day. Some days are easier than others. Through it all, show up and love.

I write that just showing up is a humble action, meaning you need humility to continue learning and growing. Parenting is a humble experience, as your children tend to be your greatest teacher. You soon realize your own wounds and you begin to hear yourself say things that your parents and grandparents once said to you—both positive and negative. To avoid the errors of the past, you need support to process those experiences and to heal old wounds.

Parenting also challenges you to articulate what you truly believe. Try explaining God to a toddler! Whatever the question, the answer always involves God's love. Teaching by storytelling and learning prayers are the first step, but most important is modeling what you preach. Our humbled actions reveal what is inside.

One of my greatest teachers is Dr. Wayne Dyer, a former professor at St. John's and world-renowned author and speaker on self-help and spirituality. He would often use a metaphor to illustrate the importance of inner work and its impact on our actions. He would ask his audience, "What happens when you squeeze an orange?"

When no one answered, he would ask flippantly, "Does apple juice come out, does pineapple juice?"

Eventually, someone would say, "Obviously, orange juice comes out when an orange is squeezed."

Dyer then explained the metaphor: "When we are squeezed in life, what is inside us will come out."

So, when you are tired and frustrated, when life squeezes you—which it certainly will, especially with the pressures of fatherhood—what is inside you will reveal itself. If you are angry and bitter, your behavior will show it, maybe by yelling or frustration. If you are sad and depressed, you might seek refuge or turn to a substance to lift your spirit.

From time to time such things will certainly happen throughout the many innings of your life, but does it happen often? What lesson are we revealing to our children in how we respond to challenges? Dyer encourages us, as do most spiritual teachers, to fill our hearts with love and peace. So, when we are squeezed, we respond with that same love and peace.

I recall an experience in my early years of supervision as a campus minister. One of my colleagues who I directly supervised made a critical error. When Dr. Pam Shea Byrnes, my mentor, supervisor, and head of the department, called him into her office, I was expecting her response to reflect the anger that I was feeling inside. Instead, she first listened. Then, with what I can only describe as "strong compassion," she became teacher to all of us. Pam explained what was necessary to correct this behavior, and she gave warning for the future. She revealed her kindness and peacefulness while upholding standards and expectations. I imagine this was the same energy Jesus exuded as he taught some of his greatest lessons by his actions. Pam taught many lessons that day, and could do so because inside her she held God's love and peace.

There are many strategies to prepare spiritually for fatherhood, but there are three at the top of my list: finding time to pray, seeking inspiration, and acting humbly. As a fellow-father, join me in reflecting on how to implement these strategies, not only as we prepare to be fathers, but throughout the varied terrains of fatherhood, the smooth and the bumpy.

Thomas Merton offers this comforting reminder: "You do not need to know precisely what is happening, or exactly where it is all going. What you need is to recognize the possibilities and challenges offered by the present moment, and to embrace them with courage, faith and hope."[32] As you accompany the mother and your unborn child into the final months of pregnancy, one chapter will close and the next one will open. This chapter started with a quote from former Los Angeles Dodgers manager, Tommy Lasorda: "Baseball is like driving, it's the one who gets home safely that counts." As a father, you are not only called to create a safe home for your family; you are also called to seek a home in the divine that dwells within. As you prepare for the first day of your child's life, quietly and slowly you are being transformed.

# Opening Day

"There is nothing like Opening Day. There's nothing like the start of a new season."[33]

—George Brett

"For this child 1 prayed, and the Lord has granted the desires of my heart."

—1 Samuel 1:27

Every winter, with great enthusiasm, 1 mark the calendar for Opening Day. After a long, cold winter in the Northeast, the green grass is a welcome sight. The pomp and circumstance of the starting line-ups, national anthem, and first pitch of the season bring me back to the game 1 so love.

Opening Day is game one of 162. The long marathon from the hope of spring, through the "dog days" of summer, climaxes—for one fortunate team—in October glory. On this first day, the world stops turning, the outside noise and work commitments are paused, and baseball takes center stage.

As a father, a different Opening Day occurs when the doctor utters those precious words, "It is time," or as 1 am putting it, "Play ball!" At that key moment, though, fathers, can only ride the bench. Sure, you will cheer with all your might, and provide support and love in the form of ice chips and holding hands, but you will likely feel helpless on the sidelines.

Like spring training, the pregnancy prepared us for this big day, as much as you can be ready. While you might not have an at-bat in this momentous occasion, you surely are called upon to step to the plate when this tiny little child rests in your shaking arms.

For some, the delivery of the baby is as smooth as it is often captured on silly television sitcoms. For others, the process of childbirth might bring its own twists and turns that leave the father praying for divine intervention. The birth of our first daughter, Shea, was anything but easy. After ninety-six hours of labor and two hours of pushing, an emergency C-section was required. I was handed blue scrubs and told to wait outside the emergency room as they prepared for surgery. I was shaking in my sneakers—I could not control my nerves. Once I was called into the room, I was invited to sit next to a hospital bed where all I could see was Suzie's head, the rest of her body behind a curtain. A nurse joined us to respond to any needs that might arise. At first, all was calm. The doctor had piped in salsa music and the chatter of the staff felt natural. Then the energy in the room suddenly changed. The nurse called for backup and several additional nurses came running into the room. Suzie turned to me and uttered, "Something is wrong. Pray." On command, I prayed like never before. The eyes of the nurse next to us changed as she stretched over the curtain to watch the doctor climb above Suzie. The baby was stuck, the umbilical cord wrapped around her neck, not once, but twice. Days later, the angelic nurse who cared for Suzie during her labor confirmed what I had feared, recapping the surgery for me and capturing the urgency of the delivery. She explained that they tried every approach to getting the baby out and that during those critical moments she too had joined me in fright and in prayer.

From behind the curtain, you can see very little so you rely on your ears. Hearing the doctor say, "I have her," was not enough. . . we didn't exhale until we heard the baby's cry. It felt like an hour, but, it must have been only a few seconds. Soon, we heard screeches from this seven-pound baby, and my heart fell back into place. The nurses cleaned her, and then swooped our baby up next to Suzie for a quick photo and a kiss. Then she was rushed to the NICU.

Before being escorted out of the room, as I kissed Suzie, I caught a glimpse of the blood spattered on the floor and the doctor's scrubs. Shortly, the doctor emerged to tell me that Suzie was heavily medicated and that the baby needed special attention. Through my tears, I thanked her. She then said, "If it was a different set of doctors and nurses, this could have been a very different story." At times these words haunt me. How quickly my life could have changed! I can only imagine the feelings of those families who do not have a happy ending, of all those mothers and children down through the generations that did not survive.

About an hour after that perilous birth, I was invited to meet our daughter. It was sobering to enter the NICU, its rooms filled with the tiniest of babies, many relying on machines to survive. Since so many of those children are sick, it was relatively quiet. Yet as I walked down the hall, I heard one baby screaming—our Shea. After I washed my hands in an impressive machine—one that we all could have used during the pandemic—I entered a small room where I introduced myself to the nurse who said, "Daddy, here is your daughter." I put my finger into the small plastic bed where she lay, her body laced with tubes. As her tiny hand clasped onto that finger and I said, "Hey there, cutie," her crying eased. The nurse turned to me and said, "She knows her daddy's voice."

And just like that, I was in love.

I am not sure what hitting a walk-off home run in Game 7 of the World Series feels like. You would have to ask Bill Mazeroski. But I cannot imagine it even coming close to the feeling of meeting your child for the first time.

There is a baseball adage that says, "There is a story behind every number on every back of every ball player." Every father has his story about the day his children were born. Like a group of retired ball players recalling their heroic wins and adventures, fathers recall the day (or days) that reigns above all others.

Never be afraid to tell your story. Share it with your children, letting them know what it was like when they played game one of their season. Tell anyone who will listen, especially young men who will be inspired by your authenticity and love.


## Let's Play Two

For a father, having a second child is like going into the postseason. You have a hunch about the extra pressure that's coming, and what's on the line. When Lily, our second daughter was born, the circumstances were different from the birth of our first. On February 29, 2020, the first reported COVID-19 death occurred in the United States. In less than two months, my hometown, Queens, New York, would soon become the world's COVID epicenter and Suzie would be entering the third trimester of her pregnancy. We realized that this baby was going to enter the world in uncharted territory.

We made the difficult decision that I would stay home with Shea, who by then was three years old. Suzie, like a pitcher closing out a pivotal game, would be all alone on the mound. It was painful for me to drop Suzie off. Fully masked and pulling her own overnight bag behind her, she entered the hospital for the scheduled C-section—alone. All I could do was pray.

Here is the reflection I wrote and shared on my website that evening:

*May 13th, 2020.*

*Today, my daughter was born.*

*I witnessed her birth, not at my wife's side, but from my home. As the Wi-Fi signal hung on for dear life, I could hear the first cries of my second child—and I was, as you say, suddenly in love.*

*I was home with my older daughter as my wife and I made this calculated and painful decision to prevent potential further infection with the COVID-19 virus. There were enough warning signs (e.g., support partners for mothers are not screened for virus) that we chose one-on-one coverage with my wife taking on the "Jordan-esque" task of a C-section, alone. Expect an ESPN special on her heroic achievements in about thirty years.*

*The months, weeks, and days leading to this life-changing moment were not easy. At times, we had to remind ourselves to feel excited as the pandemic swallowed our community. While the flashing lights and blaring sirens flying past our home have lessened, we still know what is occurring in our hospital and what is likely to follow next month.*

*In all that I was prepared to feel this day, I did not anticipate that I was going to fall in love.*

*Yes, that is all I felt as the nurse held my daughter up to my wife's iPhone. And as I soon saw her cuddle in her mother's chest, I no longer felt the fear and anxiety of the pandemic and of the C-section. I just stood in awe from 9.1 miles away.*

*God knows what the future days and weeks will bring. We will surely do our best to keep our family safe. What I do know is that on this day, there is life, and gift, and it will soon fully capture my home and heart.*

*As you likely know by now, I recently wrote a book titled, Dreams Come True. Well, my friends, this bundle of joy, her older sister, and my beloved wife are my greatest of dreams come true.*

*And while I will share with them all the love that fills my soul, these little girls will teach me lessons of life and of the heart.*

*The greatest of lessons this day is what our new addition reminded me of: to keep my eyes open for God's love.*

*I pray we all can bring this perspective into our tomorrows. From the birth of a child, to the kind gesture of a friend, to the listening ear of a trusted companion, to the settling of the sun into the darkness, love and miracles abound.*

*It is through these eyes that we are meant to see the world.*

*A final thought:*

*When I woke up yesterday morning, my first thought was the Psalm: "This is the day the Lord has made, Rejoice and be Glad in it" (118:24).*

*The Psalms are not usually my first thought—that tends to belong to the coffee that needs to quickly brew in the kitchen.*

*I consider this thought a gift, a gentle prayer that God rested in my heart on the day my baby was born. I pray that I will remember to rejoice and to be glad— even amid a pandemic filled with fear and anxiety.*

*Thank you for all your continued prayers and please join me in falling in love with all of God's creation— especially, this little girl sent from heaven.*

Despite all the challenges and difficult circumstances that formed the backdrop to Lily's birth, my heart, like when Shea was born, was filled (and remains filled) with gratitude for the opportunity to be their dad. This saying is attributed to Babe Ruth: "Baseball was, is and always will be to me the best game in the world." As a father, I mirror this sentiment in saying, "Being a dad was, is and always will be the best gift in the world." In their eyes it is easy to see gift. I marvel that they resemble both me and Suzie (unfortunately they drew the short straw in taking on more of my facial characteristics). Their quirkiness and gestures remind me of loved ones, both living and passed. How they see the world and react to the simplest of gestures adds to my devotion.

A dear friend often says, "Jimmy, you are in trouble. They have you wrapped around their little fingers." To which I respond, "I am blessed among women," a line I stole from a colleague who is the father of six beautiful girls. A beautiful thought attributed to medieval mystic and theologian, Meister Eckhart, sums up how I feel about fatherhood: "If the only prayer we ever say in our lives is 'thank you,' that will be enough."[34] There is much to be thankful for in life, and at the top of this list is the gift of my wife and my daughters. I truly am blessed among women, and I am confident that you will be as well with the children entrusted to you.

## Around the Horn

When children are entrusted to your care, they become your greatest priority. Raising them in love is one of the most important things you will do in this precious life. God's call does not begin or end with your children, however. With a divided and hurting world, there is no shortage of prayers for you to answer. The COVID-19 pandemic illustrated this on a local and global scale as the vulnerable and marginalized were disproportionately impacted. Grave injustices affect underserved communities: among many other issues here and around the world, there are rising food and housing insecurities, frequent wars and violence and increased mental health needs. No wonder we need baseball just to get through the day. But God does not want you just to get through this day or this life. God has equipped you with unique gifts and talents to serve others and to remind them of the unconditional love of our Creator. Each of us is called to live with and for one another.

Jesus offers this prayer to his heavenly Father before he is arrested and sentenced to death on the cross:

> *I ask not only on behalf of these, but also on behalf of those who will believe in me through their word, that they may all be one. As you, Father, are in me and I am in you, may they also be in us, so that the world may believe that you have sent me. The glory that you have given me I have given them, so that they may be one, as we are one, I in them and you in me, that they may become completely one, so that the world may know that you have sent me and have loved them even as you have loved me. (Jn 17: 20-23)*

Before Jesus suffered unjust violence and death, he asks God in prayer that we may be one, as he and the Father are one. Built on divine love, this prayer binds us and moves us forward. We can understand the importance of the unity Jesus prays for through baseball. Teams that succeed over the demands of a 162-game season often have a chemistry that keeps the players focused on their mission. We see this in all levels of professional and amateur baseball. Unity is contagious. The game itself requires teamwork. Throughout the nine innings, the nine players—especially the pitcher and the catcher—must work together to score as many runs as they can while keeping the opposing team from scoring. One of my favorite baseball episodes is the 5-4-3 "around the horn" double play. For those unfamiliar, for a 5-4-3 there must be a runner on first when the batter hits the ball to the third baseman, who throws to the second baseman, who ahead of the runner from first steps on his base for the first out, then throws to the first baseman before the batter reaches first. It requires multiple players catching the ball, throwing it accurately, and moving the body with precision. If any of the fielders fail in this careful sequence, the runners are safe and the pitcher is in a pickle. This unitive defensive play serves as a metaphor for life. Depending on one another is not negative, as it often feels in an individualistic society. Succeeding takes a collective approach, one that requires practice and communication. Baseball players spend a month in spring training honing these skills and rehearsing what to do in specific in-game circumstances. A pivotal double play in October began in early February on a Florida or Arizona practice field.

You, too, are called to prepare. Strengthen your relationship with God and build up your faith. Communicate with others, responding to the needs of those who your community does not treat properly and talk frequently with those you are called to serve. In these conversations, identify the needs and imagine creative solutions together. In my book, *Dreams Come True: Discovering God's Vision for Your Life*, I offer a four-step process to guide this re-imagination.

St. Paul tells us "If one member suffers, all suffer together with it; if one member is honored, all rejoice together with it" (1 Cor 12:26). By accepting our connectedness and claiming our responsibility to one another, we too can rejoice in this game of life.

We began this chapter with a focus on the glorious days when your children were born. Perhaps the divine never shines so clearly as on those days. And we conclude with the mandate to love—not only our own children, but every member of God's creation, be it neighbor or stranger, visible or invisible. Tertullian described such a life perfectly when he noted what Romans said about the early Christians in Carthage: "See how they love one another."[35] The early Christians understood how to live and how to treat each day as if it was both Opening Day and Game 7 of the World Series.

## 6th Inning

# Painful Loss

"There are three things you can do in a baseball game. You can win, or you can lose, or it can rain."[36]

—Casey Stengel

"Even though I walk through the valley of the shadow of death, I will fear no evil, for you are with me; your rod and your staff comfort me."

—Psalm 23:4

Every baseball season will have losing streaks, injuries, and conflict. The players and teams that succeed learn and grow from the pain and suffering. Each life includes the same invitation for transformation. Inevitably wounds will come, as well as God's gentle hand to meet you there. And wounds connected to your children can cut the deepest. Richard Rohr writes, "In the practical order of life, if we have never loved deeply or suffered deeply, we are unable to understand spiritual things at any depth."[37] This chapter begins with a story about one of my deepest wounds. I share it in solidarity with my fellow wounded fathers, but also to show how our pain can invite us to a deeper spiritual life and relationship with God.

In December of 2019, I sat in a New Orleans sports bar watching the hometown Saints play in Tampa Bay. A few weeks before, I rejoined the club of dads-to-be. During the commercials, I was drafting a first version of this book, which I envisioned as a prayer book for expecting dads. In mapping out the chapters of this new project, I realized that for some fathers, their child would not be born. I later learned that around fifteen percent of pregnancies end in a miscarriage. That had never happened to me, but I knew I had to address such a loss in some way, because some dads-to-be might use this book to prepare for losing a child prematurely. I left such grief as a question to examine later.

Just over three weeks later, I unexpectedly found myself in that painful category. As the doctor spoke the words, "This isn't a healthy baby," the world crashed around us. I will never forget sitting in the parking lot, holding my wife, tears streaming down our cheeks. We had planned to be holding a sonogram to put on the fridge. Instead, we held on to one another.

For the next six weeks, I suffered. I sought consolation down a variety of avenues, but nothing could fill up the loss. Between meetings I would sit at my office desk and burst into tears. There was so much to process. I felt deeply for Suzie. I was moved by her strength and grace. She had wanted so badly to be pregnant, and this loss took a physical and emotional toll. Following the news of the miscarriage, the doctor told Suzie that within a week she would need a dilation and curettage (D&C) procedure. There was now this agonizing waiting period. As she prepared for the procedure, Suzie told me, in a tender voice, "I want this to be over, but at the same time, I don't want to let go." I suffered with her, yet not fully experiencing her agony.

I felt for Shea. She did not know about the baby or the miscarriage, but she sensed something was different. On the day we found out, when I picked her up from day care I just had to hold onto her a little tighter. I felt for our family and friends, who mourned and prayed from a distance. They respected the space we needed to let this devastating news penetrate our heads and our hearts

I wondered about this child (I had a deep sense that she was a girl) and who she would have been. I started to imagine what she would have looked like, how she would have acted, who from our past she would have reminded me of. I then started to wonder about her soul, trusting she was with our loved ones who already had transitioned. I prayed through her to God to find peace in my broken heart.

Throughout this book, I playfully connect the journey of fatherhood with the game of baseball. In this chapter, it feels inappropriate. Any metaphor of a losing streak or injury cannot represent the pain of a lost child, even one who dies only a few weeks after conception.

## Bereavement List

In revisiting my own story for this chapter, I discovered four factors that helped me heal. I pray that if you too must carry such a cross, or have a cross now weighing you down, these words will help heal the hurt and soothe the pain. What I share may apply to all who are grieving the loss of loved ones, no matter their age or place in your life.

The first is prayer. We didn't tell many people about the miscarriage, but for those who knew, I could sense their prayer carrying us through our grief. My empty cup was filling up with love and compassion. This experience showed me the importance of following up on prayers I had promised. On social media posts or in text messages or during conversations, I often say "praying for you" to suffering friends. In that moment I often say a silent prayer, but I know I can do more.

After receiving prayers of healing, I learned the importance of sending love and spiritually uniting with my fellow companions on this journey. To my daily prayer routine, I added time to reflect on those I encountered that day, the prayers I pledged, and who could benefit from my love.

The second factor that helped in my healing was the kindness of so many. My colleagues who responded with love, my family and friends who sent thoughtful messages, the doctors and nurses who understood the pain of this journey—all these made the time easier. Even those who did not know the specifics but could see my tired eyes and sense my heavy heart offered a gentle hand of support. This experience reminded me to be aware of those who are suffering silently.

If we are honest with ourselves, we recognize that everyone bears wounds and struggles. Smiles on a face or happy images on Instagram do not tell the whole story. When you cannot understand why someone might be acting in a hurtful way, perhaps hidden wounds might be the cause. It isn't an excuse, but our world would benefit from a collective compassionate heart that leads to a love that heals. You will never know how your kindness may be answering another's prayers.

The third factor was trying to help others. I invested time into my inspirational writing. I was more attentive to the students and colleagues in need. On my walks across campus I tried to find people to help, such as a new student at the start of the semester looking for their classroom. Walking to and from work, I tried to notice people in need, such as a person asking for money or food. As I opened my eyes and changed my perspective, they turned up. They were always there; I just hadn't seen them. Our own suffering can move us to unite with others in their pain.

During this painful time, another wound began to take shape. One of my favorite uncles, my grandfather's brother, Benny, was dying. When my mom was only fifteen her dad passed away and Benny became one of the family's father-figures. Two days before our fateful doctor's appointment, Suzie and I had celebrated New Year's Eve with him. We knew his condition was going to get worse quickly, and so it did. In his final weeks I visited the hospital as much as possible to listen and to be with him and our family. On one of those visits, he woke up and realized I was sitting there. I could tell how happy he was to see me. The light in his tired eyes reminded me of all the times Uncle Benny had brightened the room when he entered with his contagious laugh. You knew how much he loved you because he told you so. Everyone just wanted to be with him. As his final days drew near, grief did not overwhelm me. I felt at home in it. I found an unexpected sense of peace in facing loss, whether it came early or late in life. I also felt relief that my child would be joined by one of her dad's favorite people.

The fourth factor was a spiritual counselor who listened to me, guided me, and invited healing into my heart. He bandaged my wounds and accompanied me through this uncharted territory. He recommended that I create something to remember my lost child. As an artist, I found that painting allowed me to mix my tears with the acrylic oil. With each brushstroke, I felt the burden lighten. That painting did not turn out to be my greatest work but is perhaps one of the most important. I hung it on the office wall near my desk where I can look at it and think of her. My counselor invited me to use a God-given talent to create a healing remedy. When I take my last breath, I look forward to reuniting with her and entering more into this great, and at times, painful mystery.

Those "four factors"—the power of prayer and kindness, the importance of spiritual healing and service, and turning to professionals to offer support and a listening ear—helped me through this difficult moment of my life. Your life experience is unique to you and your "factors" may differ, but what's important is to embrace each moment and realize that you're not alone.

Most of the stories in this book are my own. What takes place for others may differ from my experience but is no less painful. Some have lost babies further along in pregnancy, in delivery, and even after birth. Such pain cannot even be imagined, much less understood. I hope that those who have walked these painful roads find solidarity and companionship. For those who have not experienced such loss, I pray you gain greater empathy and compassion for your fellow fathers and their partners, while seeking healing and peace for the wounds you carry.

## Rally Cry

As I faced the heartbreak of the miscarriage, I yearned for a community that would understand. As men and as a society we would be better off if we talked more and created space to walk these journeys together. I felt reluctant to share my pain as it was Suzie who endured the physical loss. Like others in this role, I assumed the caretaker role for my partner as I suffered in silence. How do fathers find support for the spiritual, emotional, and psychological loss? My search for this community came up empty. I am hopeful that increased dialogue and support replaces the silence.

I did find community, however, in a spiritual support system that became a necessary gift. As mentioned earlier, I find comfort in the spiritual community of saints, those who walked before and faced similar pain and loss. My belief that we remain connected in God through the generations nourished my faith during this difficult time.

I found the most comfort in Mary, the Blessed Mother. She stood by the cross where her son faced one of the most gruesome forms of death, crucifixion. As depicted in Michelangelo's *The Pietà*, she held her lifeless son's body and afterwards, with his companions, mourned his death and rejoiced in his resurrection. Many episodes establish Mary's reputation as a mother for all. The scriptural account of her role at Cana in leading Jesus to turn water into wine shows her motherliness, but my favorite is found not in scripture but in tradition.

After Jesus ascended into heaven, Mary remained with the disciples in the upper room, where they mourned and prayed (Acts 1:14). Tradition tells us that despite her own mourning, Mary, being the strong woman and mother that she was, nurtured the disciples and urged them into action. When the Holy Spirit soon came and filled their hearts (Acts 2), she watched her son's friends and followers pick themselves up and continue to love as Jesus had taught them. There comes a time in our own grieving when we too need to return to service. There is no timetable, and we never fully heal from such a loss. It just becomes part of our story.

Turn to Mary, who points us to the cross and the resurrection. While I wish we had never experienced that miscarriage, it did make old ways die and let a new identity take shape. It was painful, but my faith did grow. I pray that I am responding with courage and love, like that which Mary modeled for her son's companions.

This chapter has presented a reality that many fathers face. Even if you are fortunate enough not to have experienced the heartbreak of a miscarriage or the loss of a child, you certainly will experience other losses and deaths in your life. At times, the burden of fatherhood will weigh heavy and it will force you to your knees in prayer. Here, in the suffering, we are invited into a deeper relationship with our God.

Chiara Lubich writes, "In life we do many things, say many things, but the voice of suffering offered out of love—which is perhaps unheard by and unknown to others—is the loudest cry that can penetrate heaven."[38] Trust that God is hearing you when the wounds are forming, that God is with you. Allow these moments to penetrate your heart, to make you feel and love deeper. In this pain, suffering and life unite and can be understood in a new way.

# Stretched

"Baseball is a hard game to play, so no matter what uniform you wear, you have something in common with the guy in the other dugout: We all fail. The game is built that way."[39]

—David Ortiz

"Beware that you don't look down on any of these little ones. For I tell you that in heaven their angels are always in the presence of my heavenly Father."

—Matthew 18:10

As we brought our first-born home, driving on the expressway as slowly as the law allowed, I wondered how the hospital could just let us leave. Suzie's aunt had agreed to help us when we brought Shea home. When she had to depart two days later, we begged her to stay. The duty of being responsible for this fragile child felt too much to bear.

Chapter 4, "Spring Training," touched on the spiritual practices in preparation for fatherhood. When it is time to raise a child, especially in those opening weeks, you need to learn countless lessons and you are humbled as the rollercoaster of this fatherhood journey begins. Our opening weeks and months included many visits to the pediatrician, above and beyond what was recommended. We were quite surprised when we got a bill from the insurance company because our visits were above our allocated annual coverage. Even greater than the unexpected medical bill was the anxiety from searching the web for every bump, rash, and behavior that set off alarms.

For example, one night, I felt a soft, almost squishy, bump on Shea's two-month-old head. The next day we rushed to the pediatrician, who said it could be something and we should monitor it. I spent many hours those next few nights looking up possibilities then recovering from nightmares about the horror stories that I read a few hours earlier. I was preparing myself for the worst. At the next visit a few weeks later, the doctor reassured us that the bump was smaller in size and probably just a fluid build-up from the difficult delivery. She then said, "It was never something to worry about." I was too relieved to care, but I sure wish I had those lost hours back. The humbling lessons continued in those opening months as I learned about diapers, wipes, creams, and so much more. In all of it, I felt a reverence as I tended to this precious child entrusted to my care, while at the same time, I was learning how to be her father.

## A Shift

As a student of psychology, I appreciate what Sigmund Freud said: "I cannot think of any need in childhood as strong as the need for a father's protection."[40] I would expand this to include mothers, as I knew from the college students I have been accompanying that a compassionate and loving parent creates a safe and confident foundation. Unfortunately, many were struggling with parents, especially fathers, who were either absent or extremely hard on their children. The issues varied, but it was no surprise that when our conversations turned spiritual they couldn't relate to or believe in God as a compassionate and unconditionally loving Father.

In my office, I have made it a point to display a print of Rembrandt's *The Return of the Prodigal Son* behind my chair, opposite the miscarriage-inspired painting, I use this image as a teaching tool to introduce or reinforce God's love for God's children. My book, *Dreams Come True: Discovering God's Vision for Your Life*, devotes an entire chapter to this painting, the parable it illustrates, and the story behind how it was given to me by a dear friend who brought it from Rome.

The parable, taken from the Gospel of Luke (15:11-32), is well-known. Jesus explains that the younger son asks for his inheritance, which would be equivalent to asking that his father be dead. That son spends all the money, only to face starvation during a great famine. He returns to his father, not to seek reconciliation, as he did not expect it, but simply to survive by working for his father. In some versions of this story from other traditions, the son forgets who he is. Only when the father sends people to find him does he remember. Sometimes, we may have similar experiences in which people come into our lives and remind us who we are and who we belong to.

In Luke's account, overwhelmed with joy upon seeing his son in the distance, the father runs to him. He tells the servants to kill the fatted calf, as there will be a celebration. His son receives a ring, new clothes, and is welcomed home with open arms. Later that night, returning from work, the older son sees the party going on. Finding out that his younger brother has returned, he is furious. He had been faithful to his father, working hard on the land, only to see his brother welcomed after squandering his inheritance. When the older son presses the father, the father responds, "But we had to celebrate and rejoice, because this brother of yours was dead and has come to life; he was lost and has been found" (Lk 15:32).

In Rembrandt's painting the father and the older son resemble one another. They are dressed in the same robes and have long beards. However, in his book of the same name, *The Return of the Prodigal Son*, Henri Nouwen points out some important differences. [41] The father's hands are open, whereas the older brother's hands are closed. The father embraces the son kneeling before him. The father's eyes, which appear to be blind, allow not a human gaze, but a divine one.

New fathers find it easy to see the divine spark in their infant children. In return, the children see our spark, perhaps as bright as it has ever been. Unfortunately, as their children grow, fathers might begin to impose their own expectations and their love can be misunderstood as conditional.

Consider your relationship with your own earthly father and father figures. Do you feel unconditionally loved by them? What about God? Do you feel God's unconditional love? Can you truly believe and accept it? Knowing and believing you are loved, no matter what, grounds your self-perception and your well-being. Such unconditional love generates a sense of security in this world, and in the next. The challenge of fatherhood is to work not only on your relationship with your own father, your father-figures, and God the Father, but also to be a father. Your actions and words shape the next generation.

Surely what you may have said to your children echoes what your father, and perhaps your father's father, has said to you. For better or for worse, learned behavior gets repeated. If you are aware of this, you can replicate what is grounded in love, not what is bound in inner pain. Such self-awareness requires healthy reflection and conversation. It involves accepting that your formation is neither all good nor all bad, but fully human. Can you see with eyes of the father in *The Return of the Prodigal Son*, acknowledging both the past and the future? Can you love unconditionally? Like the best of managers, not only must you teach and create accountability, you also must nurture your children on their terms. Longtime Detroit Tigers manager, Sparky Anderson, said, "Baseball is a simple game. If you have good players and keep them in the right frame of mind, then the manager is a success."[42] What's true for managers is true for fathers.

## Ya Gotta Believe

The spiritual call to fatherhood is to foster such acceptance and love in children, and the right frame of mind requires an evolving and maturing faith life. Parents' critical responsibility is to raise children to have their own relationship with God. Understanding their own moral and faith development guides this education. For two decades I have taught theology and explained scripture, but when I ponder how to explain God to my own children, I pause and wonder how to proceed. How do you guide and form a child to accept the mystery of God and God's love? How do you help your child understand an incarnational God, always present in all things? How do your actions model your words? From the golden rule to messages of love and service, does your behavior reinforce the lesson? What about your prayer life? How do you teach your children to be in relationship with God?

When I was a child, I recall going to church, sitting in the same pew that we occupied each week during the 10:30 a.m. Mass. I remember looking up to my dad as he held the missal and recited prayers with the larger community.

He didn't tell me to pray, he showed me how to pray.

His calmness revealed the power of prayer.

His seriousness revealed the nature of prayer.

I remember my mom praying her rosary every night, followed by prayers and novenas to various saints, especially Mary. It was a part of her routine. I remember seeing not just her discipline, but how much it meant to her to say those words and to reconnect with God.

Every spring semester, I interview high school seniors for the Catholic Scholars program at St. John's University. My colleagues and I meet with over a hundred students, learning more about the hopes they have for their college experience. We have the almost impossible task of selecting a cohort of thirty from very strong and dedicated candidates. One question we always ask is, "Tell us about your prayer life." It is moving to hear the students discuss their parents and grandparents, how they pray together at Mass, before dinner, or in the car. They are not ashamed by this; rather, they are proud and thankful for their families which shaped them in holiness. In an unexpectedly and frequently difficult world, teaching your children how to be in relationship with God is one of the greatest gifts you can give them.

## Free Agents

Hall of Famer Willie Stargell said, "To me, baseball has always been a reflection of life. Like life, it adjusts. It survives everything." Fatherhood requires constant adjustment, especially because children are free to develop their own identity—which probably will differ from that of their old man.

In my graduate studies for counseling, one of my professors told us that by saying "no" for the first time, a child begins to create his or her own identity. As parents, we are charged to choreograph that cautious dance of creating parameters while maintaining freedom and room for creativity. That dance includes many pitfalls. Take your child's name for example. Many children begin life bearing a label, a name that represents a parent or cherished family member, friend, or saint. There isn't an explicit expectation that the child live up to the name, but there are plenty of implicit messages and hopes that your child will reflect the positive traits of that namesake.

Just take a stroll to your local Little League field and watch the fathers, some of them trying in their child to relive past glory or seek unachieved success. Inevitably, there will be a dad or two who isn't there just to enjoy his kid having fun and playing a game. They want to see their "mini-me" in action. During my own Little League days, some dads would yell at the umpire or the coach (whether for their kid's team or the opponent's). Sometimes the yelling elevated into a parking lot brawl. The unresolved issues of angry men darkened the purity of the game.

Many frustrated men with unfulfilled childhood dreams feel burdened and disrespected by their employers or families. Many see the clock of their life ticking and wonder what could have been had they taken different roads. Such regrets and disappointments can shape how they raise their children, not wanting them to make the same mistakes, or any mistake at all. As a result, they do not leave their children free to create, to form, to discover. The children are not free to strike out or to make errors. They may feel the burden of not disappointing their parents. Over my almost two decades of ministry with college students, this is by far my most common conversation. Many struggle with their academic pursuits, feeling pressure to pursue a career or stay in a major that is their parents' dream, not theirs. Some do change paths, but most bear with it until they no longer can, their frustration often manifesting itself in unhealthy decisions and life patterns.

On the other hand, many feel they have permission to be free—to pursue and chase their dreams. They still wrestle with parental messages from their past and present, but that tension does not control them. Hall of Famer Ted Williams sums up students' tension between parental expectations and their own freedom: "Baseball is the only field of endeavor where a man can succeed three times out of ten and be considered a good performer."[43] If you can take this same approach with your children, celebrating where they do succeed while inviting them to learn from the outs of life, you will leave the next generation with leaders and people of faith who better reflect the compassion of our God.

In closing, let's look at a cautionary tale from baseball. Bill Buckner was a career .289 hitter who played for five teams over his twenty-two-year career.[44] Despite being a batting champion and an All Star, he is remembered for his crucial Game 6 error in the bottom of the tenth inning of the 1986 World Series between the Boston Red Sox and the New York Mets. With the game tied, Buckner allowed a slow ground ball off the bat of the Mets' Mookie Wilson to trickle under his glove and into right field. Ray Knight ran home with the winning run. Minutes prior, the Red Sox were a strike away from winning their first World Series since trading away Babe Ruth and winning the title in 1918. Buckner became the poster child for the "Curse of the Bambino." The following season, the Red Sox released Buckner, then in 1990 he rejoined the team for a short stint. Although he received a warm welcome upon his return, his error was never forgotten.

The Red Sox finally won the championship in 2004, breaking the curse. They won it again in 2007 (as well as 2013 and 2018). In April of 2008, when the Sox raised their championship banner at the home opener in Fenway Park, Buckner was invited to throw out the first pitch. He received a two-minute standing ovation from the sold-out crowd. After the game Buckner said, "I really had to forgive, not the fans of Boston, per se, but I would have to say in my heart I had to forgive the media for what they put me and my family through. So, you know, I've done that and I'm over that."[45]

After that fateful night in 1986, Buckner received death threats. One of Boston's heroes was alienated and persecuted because of one play in a baseball game. And you have to wonder... If the Sox had never gone on to win a title, if the "Curse of the Bambino" remained in effect, would the Red Sox nation have ever welcomed him home?

In 2019 Bill Buckner passed away at the age of sixty-nine.

There are many similar stories of division, hurt, and loss between parents and children. Children make mistakes, take different roads, claim identities that their parents do not accept, leading to further pain and distance. If there is a schism, parents need to take a deep dive into their heart, explore their relationship with their children, and seek unity. Buckner had his healing moment, but only after twenty-plus years of suffering. Accept your children, whether they win or lose, and applaud them with the standing ovation they deserve by way of affirmations, freedom, and love. May your children know that you back them up, no matter their errors. Like the merciful father from the parable of the Prodigal Son, may your children know they can always return home.

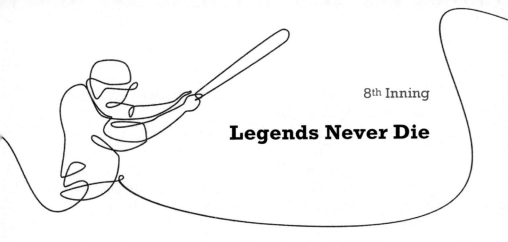

# Legends Never Die

"Love is the most important thing in the world. But baseball is pretty good too."[46]

—Yogi Berra

"In the way of righteousness there is life; along that path is immortality."

—Proverbs 12:28

In the classic baseball film, *The Sandlot*, a fictional Babe Ruth tells Benny "The Jet" Rodriguez, "Remember kid, there's heroes and there's legends; heroes get remembered but legends never die." As baseball fans, we celebrate those who wear our colors and transcend heroic success to become legends. As spiritual people, we look to legendary individuals who have lived extraordinary lives. Throughout history, teachers, prophets, healers, and saints have come to be called legends.

Pope Francis reminds us, "To be saints is not a privilege for the few, but a vocation for everyone."[47] The vocation of fatherhood is a call to legendary status, to sainthood. Your children may wear a professional team's jersey with someone else's name on the back, but it is yours that they will carry with them for the rest of their lives.

To your child, you are called to be legendary—but what does this look like?

The backs of baseball cards include a player's statistics—his achievements and generosity etched in time. The saints and spiritual leaders leave their legacy in their writings and actions, in the communities they founded and the miracles that occurred during and after their lives.

As fathers, you are called to be your children's legends. You are not called to be perfect, but you are called to shower them with the same unconditional love that God shows to each of us.

One night I was giving Shea a bath. She was four at the time, and as four-year-olds do, her imagination was running as wild as the A's Rickey Henderson on the basepaths. She told me how when she was older she wanted to become a mermaid and asked if I would come visit her when she called the ocean her new home. I played along, saying I would certainly come visit but since I wasn't a mermaid, I couldn't live with her under the water. At that moment, with her big blue eyes watering up, she looked at me and said, "What if I don't remember you?"

Talk about a punch to the gut.

I turned my head, attempting to regain composure. Holding in the tears I mumbled, "You will never forget me, and I will never forget you." Then, feeling the seriousness of the moment weighing greater than I could handle, I suggested a different solution.

"Don't worry Shea," I said. "I will just become a mermaid so we can be together."

She responded, "You can't be a mermaid dad, you are too old."

*How will your children remember you?*

This question is your mission statement for your precious vocation as a father.

This chapter will present three dimensions of becoming legendary, and the skills you need to do so. They may not seem to fit the "masculine" images that society paints for men and fathers, but I am not attempting to be controversial. Rather, I seek to expand the parameters that many fathers feel they must operate within. Any guy who has been told "be a man" understands the explicit and implicit messages about fatherhood that shape our perspective and operations.

I suggest these three skills:

- Increased Patience
- Non-judgmental Listening
- Expressed Emotions

In previous chapters I reviewed the importance of prayer as a foundation for all our vocations. Born out of prayer are these attributes that will leave a great impact on your children and world. Let's explore these attributes.

## Increased Patience

A famous quote on patience is attributed to St. Francis de Sales: "Have patience with all things, but, first, with yourself." You should post it on the bathroom mirror so you can begin and end each day with this reminder. Everyone would benefit from it—especially yourself. The great pressures on fathers are reflected in their ever-growing to-do lists. The weight of your many demands can cause you not only to overlook the gifts in your midst, but can easily make you cranky and angry. Holding the world on your shoulders is exhausting.

God does not ask you to do this. Shift your perspective by letting go of the desire to do it all, be it all, control it all. Just let God be God. It sounds simple, but the challenge of letting go and being patient with the Lord will last your lifetime. The Book of Proverbs reminds us: "In their hearts humans plan their course, but the LORD establishes their steps" (16:9). Similarly, in the *Tao Te Ching,* Lao-Tzu writes: "Do you have patience to wait till your mud settles and the water is clear?"[48] The journey of fatherhood, like life, will have straight or broken paths, and muddy or clear water. Being patient with yourself, and at times with God, allows yourself, and those who live and work with you, to experience greater peace. Being patient with yourself might feel as difficult as hitting a Jacob DeGrom four-seam fastball, but it is a spiritual challenge worth pursuing.

If St. Francis de Sales had focused just on being a dad, perhaps he would have said: "Have patience with all things, but, first, with yourself, and second, your children and your partner." You need patience to handle what my wife calls the many "roommate issues" that inevitably surface when you share a home and a life. Patience is even more essential not only for allowing God to be God, but for allowing your partner and children to be themselves.

Your children are not here to correct your mistakes, or to fulfill your hopes and dreams. God made them with your DNA, but with their own purpose. Support them as they discover what God planted on their hearts. Cultivate their talents as they are revealed.

Try not to make them understand; rather, work tire-lessly to understand them—even if doing so is difficult. Surely they will remind you of yourself in some ways, but avoid the temptation to presume that they are identical to you. You will create obstacles that they will spend years climbing to meet your expectations instead of their own. Be patient as they learn and grow, accompany them by showing love and support. This does not mean you cannot teach them or offer guidance and wisdom. Do all of that, but then let them be. Let them ask questions, make mistakes and make their own choices. If your children remember you as a patient man, you will have given them an immeasurable gift.

## Non-judgmental Listening

As a minister I learned a most important lesson from my pastor when we were trying to establish a dynamic youth ministry program. At the start of our planning meetings with the leadership team he would say: "Remember, every person has a story to tell. They just don't always have someone to listen." This became the focus of our ministry. We created space for community, we found ways to serve and to pray, but the heart of what we did was listening.

This insight has served me well as a father. I try to create a space where my children are heard so they can always share their story—no matter how trying it may be at that particular moment. This task is difficult, and a daily challenge. Our home is alive with energy and sounds, from the cries of hunger to the soundtrack of Disney classics playing on loop. It's never quiet. In addition to the sounds that make up the backdrop of our lives, there are all the sounds and sentences that our children communicate. Especially during the toddler years, it often feels as if we are playing a friendly game of ten thousand questions. Then add in the endless distractions, including, but not limited to, our phones, computer, tablets, television, and music. It is easier to get lost in these devices than to open my ears and heart to my children and partner.

As I listen to my children, I am reminded of how much they can teach me. I must listen daily to gain insight into their little hearts. They, in return, remind me of how to be their dad and how to prioritize what matters most. Seeing the world through their crystal blue eyes invites me to a simpler perspective. They inspire me to grow in love.

For example, as toddlers both Shea and Lily would cry if I hurt a fly—literally! On one occasion when Lily was twenty months old, her bottom lip curled over, and tears flowed down her cheeks as I "removed" a fly who unexpectedly joined us for dinner. She looked at me with disappointment and sadness, confused at how I didn't value that life.

I imagine as they both continue to transform, I will transform as well. I hope to learn from their kindness, their exploration, and their relationship with God. They will teach me how to accompany them, and I will guide their way with the wisdom that I, too, was allowed to freely discover.

Truly being able to listen to your children may well be the most important dimension of fatherhood. A conscious effort to be fully present to your family will build confidence and trust. Once you have developed strategies to allow for listening (e.g., we have a no electronic rule at our dinner table), listen without judgement, listen with love. According to the Dalai Lama, "Love is the absence of judgement." Listening without judgement is a challenge, especially for a parent. Not only does the drive to protect and to control impede listening, but it can also cause you to issue decisive orders that close the lines of communication.

I recall positive examples from my teenage years, especially during dinner conversations with my family where I was given space to share my career aspirations. From my high school through college years, I dipped into art, journalism, psychology, and then ministry. Those dinner conversations were filled with support and nourishment. My parents invested in the art supplies I needed for my classes. They bought me a laptop for my writing, and they helped me choose a college where I could learn and grow.

I imagine they may have bit their tongue when they wanted to suggest that I pursue a more stable and lucrative field or fought the temptation to pressure me to fit their expectations. This was most evident during the three hot summer months after I turned sixteen, when I worked for my dad's electrical company. Early on my first morning, my dad met me at the kitchen table and he handed me a mug of coffee. The mug bore his name, which is the same as mine, printed under the image of a lightbulb. At the that moment I felt more like I was embarking on a rite of passage than beginning a summer job. My father built this business, and he was extremely successful. Working with him helped me realize not only how gifted he was in his trade, but also how hard this job was, especially in the extreme summer heat and the bitter winter cold. I also quickly realized that I was not cut out to be an electrician. On my first day, while sweeping up a basement after a more seasoned co-worker had completed the electrical project, I raised the broom handle too high and shattered several fluorescent lights hanging below the dropped ceiling. As the shards of glass came showering down with my father and the homeowner looking on, I knew it was going to be a very long summer.

My career goals led me to different pursuits, but my father (and mother) always supported me. Whatever judgement or disappointment he did feel, he did not let it come across the dining room table when he passed the mashed potatoes. I received only support and love. I do not take this for granted; many of my friends had very different experiences. As a father now, I try to do the same for my children, to let them shine their lights as only they can!

## Expressed Emotions

In the hit film *A League of Their Own*, Tom Hanks's character Jimmy Dugan, the fictional manager of an all-women baseball team famously said, "There's no crying in baseball." Men often receive a similar message: "There's no crying in life."

Expressing emotion is complicated, influenced by cultural norms and societal pressures. How to act and how you handle your emotions comes from what you were taught and what was modelled for you. If your father expressed his anger by throwing things or punching walls, you may feel the urge to do the same—especially when stressed and squeezed by life. If your male authority figures never spoke about emotions, it is likely that you will struggle or resist to share with others how you feel. On the other hand, if authority figures, including your father, showed emotions appropriately and allowed you to do the same, it is likely that you are more comfortable sharing your own feelings. Most of us have had authority figures who modeled both, shaping your thoughts as you built your worldview and place within it.

I have found that when men suppress their emotions they become manifested in negative behaviors like addiction, aggression, and irresponsible behavior. Those who struggle with an addiction like alcohol may seek help and community from a program like Alcoholics Anonymous (AA), where they must confront what has chained them and prevented freedom and authenticity. AA encourages members to follow twelve steps that lead to a life of sobriety and health. Many, such as Honesty [Step 1], Surrender [Step 3], and Acceptance [Step 6] are connected to emotions. AA is founded upon a dependence on a Higher Power. In his book, *Divine Therapy and Addiction: Centering Prayer and the Twelve Steps*, Thomas Keating writes "[In AA] you are just open to the possibility that God is not the way you think God is from your particular cultural background or human experience thus far."[49] This changed perspective on God, who due to socialization and scriptural references is often seen as a male figure, lets participants take a new approach to expressing emotions. Keating continues, "We know that whatever happens, the love of God is always with us and that [God] will turn our failures into perfect love."[50]

Expressing emotion can feel like a failure to "live up" to the standards set by an invisible collective. Not only can the expression of emotion seem negative (e.g., crying), so can the cause of the emotion (e.g., broken heart, loss of job, etc.). Expressing emotion invites you to an authentic freedom, a faithfulness to your true self. Thomas Merton writes, "Only when we are able to 'let go' of everything within us, all desire to see, to know, to taste and to experience the presence of God, do we truly become able to experience that presence with the overwhelming conviction and reality that revolutionize our entire inner life."[51] Experiencing the presence of God, be it in the heartaches of life or in the eyes of our children, gives us the freedom to simply be God's beloved.

When we deal with our emotions only by suppressing them, we are keeping God out of the situation and out of our lives. Because we come from God, including all that we feel, we are better served to seek God in those emotions instead of denying ourselves the right to feel what is surfacing. Bring this to prayer, seek counsel, and find the freedom to reveal and accept your emotions. This provides not only a greater freedom and a deeper relationship with God, but also gives your children permission to do the same.

Although it is often frowned upon for men to show emotions—especially tears—in public, when done at certain moments it is revered. During the induction speeches at the Baseball Hall of Fame tears flow as the players recall their parents and most significant coaches and teammates. Perhaps the most memorable baseball speech of all time was Lou Gehrig's farewell, delivered at Yankee Stadium between games of a July 4, 1939 doubleheader with the Washington Senators. Gehrig had been diagnosed with amyotrophic lateral sclerosis (ALS), what is now often called Lou Gehrig disease. Not only was his career ending, but also his life. He passed away within two years.

Gehrig, the Yankees' "Iron Horse," approached the microphone that day wiping the tears from his eyes with his handkerchief.[52] Any true baseball fan can recall the words that followed: "Fans, for the past two weeks you have been reading about the bad break I got. Yet today I consider myself the luckiest man on the face of this earth." Consider the scene: ballplayers surrounding him at home plate, tens of thousands in the stands and countless more listening on their radios. Echoing through time, a man was showing authentic emotion. Our children, our world would be better served by more examples of men who are willing to reveal what lives in their hearts.

Every father can blaze a legendary path. You have the opportunity, in all your vocations and in all your relationships, to reflect the love of God. If you seek increased patience, present non-judgmental listening, and express your emotions in a healthy fashion, you will be remembered for your authenticity, your kindness, and your love.

# Happy Recap

"A life is not important except in the impact it has on other lives." [53]

— Epitaph on Jackie Robinson's tombstone

"And we know that in all things God works for the good of those who love him, who have been called according to his purpose."

—Romans 8:28

B ob Murphy, the Hall of Fame broadcaster and voice of the Mets from 1962 to 2003, used to end each of his team's victories with a "happy recap," summarizing the key plays and heroes. There will come a day, after you take your last breath, when your children and loved ones will recall your life. This will occur in eulogies, reflections around the dinner table, and in shared memories as they look through photographs, videos, and relics that you once wore or used.

Will their memories result in a happy recap?

This is up to you, in how you live and love. It is also up to others in how they live and love in return. As you have read through this book, I pray you have seen this vocation, if it is what God has called you to fulfill, as your greatest of responsibilities. Fathers possess remarkable power in shaping their children's lives. Although it is easy for this to get lost in the business of the day, you are challenged to live in each moment in the present, always teaching, modeling, and loving.

You'll never be perfect at this task—that is not achievable. Along the way you will hit your home runs, but you will also swing and miss. The difference is that when you do strike out, when you are charged with errors, you make them into teachable moments where you reveal how to seek forgiveness, to create peace, to find remedies, to always act out of love.

Jill McDonough's beautiful poem "We're Human Beings" captures our solidarity with those who make mistakes, which reminds us of the humanity we all share:

> *That's why we're here*, said Julio Lugo
> to the *Globe*. Sox fans booed
> poor Lugo, booed his at-bat after
> he dropped the ball in the pivotal fifth.
> *That ball, I got to it, I just*
> *couldn't come up with it.*
> Lugo wants you to know
> he is fast: a slower player
> wouldn't even get close
> enough to get booed. Lugo
> wants you to know he's only
> human: *We're human beings.*
> *That's why we're here. If not,*
> *I would have wings.*
> *I'd be beside God right now.*
> *I'd be an angel.*
> *But I'm not an angel.*
> *I'm a human being that lives right here.*

Next day, all is forgiven. Lugo's home run, Lugo's
sweet comment to the press.
I wanted to make a poster like the ones that say
*It's my birthday!* or *First Time at Fenway!*
   or, pathetic, *ESPN.*
Posterboard, permanent marker to say
*Lugo: me, too.*
*I'm a human being that lives right here,* decided
it's too esoteric, too ephemeral a reference,
   but it's true:
Oh, Lugo, Julio Lugo, I'm here with you.[54]

While you hope that those you love will be sharing
a happy recap of your life, what matters slightly more is
how you stand before our God. Maybe it will be like a
scene in the classic baseball film, *Field of Dreams,* when
the "Shoeless" Joe Jackson character, staring at the
backyard sandlot carved out of the cornfields, asks Ray
Kinsella, "Is this heaven?"

Kinsella famously responds, "No, it's Iowa."

I cannot imagine what my encounter with God
will be like when I, God willing, return home, but just
as Shoeless Joe sees heaven in his baseball refuge, I
glimpse it in the eyes of my children. When my toddler wraps her arms around my neck, I too have asked
myself "Is this heaven?" Times like that inspire me to
pray over what would make my life's recap a happy one
in the "eyes" of God. What will matter most?

It will not be meeting deadlines or keeping up with
internal and external expectations. It will not be the
size of my bank account, my home, my waistline, or my
car. It surely will not be in how many awards and acco-

lades I receive. All that matters is how I loved, especially toward those who call me by that precious name: "Dad."

Baseball loyalty often gets passed down through the generations. My father was neutral about the Mets and Yankees (as a lefty, though, Mickey Mantle was his hero when he was a kid), but his father was a broken-hearted Brooklyn Dodgers fan. When the Dodgers moved to California in 1957, he waited patiently for National League baseball to return to New York. In 1962, his prayers were answered in the Mets.

I was only eight years old when Grandpa Walters went home to God. Some memories have stood the test of time, but most of what I know is from stories about him and the legacy that formed his son, and as a result, me. When I was sixteen, during that summer when I worked for my dad, an unanticipated experience united me and my grandfather. It was the day's final job, a couple in their sixties who needed some electrical work that I likely did not comprehend. I remember walking into this warm space. Light jazz music from a record player and a delicious smell coming from the kitchen set the ambiance. A gentleman approached me, stuck out his hand and welcomed me into his home. He then shared that he knew my grandfather from their service together during the Korean War.

That connection made my grandpa's spirit come alive within me. In this stranger's house, I felt home. My memories were limited of my grandfather, but here in his friend's home, I sensed his presence. I soaked in the experience, trying to capture this precious encounter—I can still smell the dinner being prepared in the kitchen. Although I do not remember what else he said that day,

I remember how welcomed he made me feel. As I am creating a home for my own family, I often think of this encounter as I am preparing dinner and country music (my grandfather's favorite) is playing from our streaming device. I think of that summer afternoon, and in some small way I attempt to recreate that feeling and that connection, sensing that my grandfather is united with me and with his great-grandchildren in our late afternoon ritual.

I wrote much of this book during the COVID-19 pandemic. It was a challenging time that shoved us all into a new reality. For some, like myself, I became a father again during this trying year and I sought inspiration in familiar and new voices. One such voice was Irish poet and theologian, John O'Donohue. His reflections, greatly influenced by mystical teachings and Celtic spirituality, are food for the soul. One of his books, *To Bless the Space Between Us: A Book of Blessings*, contains a passage that captures the transformation generated by fatherhood. Although this blessing is titled "For a Father," it invites all of us to recall the miracle of our vocations and to find rest in our trust in God:

> As the shimmer of dawn transforms the night
> Into a blush of color futured with delight,
> The eyes of your new child awaken in you
> A brightness that surprises your life.
>
> Since the first stir of its secret becoming,
> The echo of your child has lived inside you,
> Strengthening through all its night of forming
> Into a sure pulse of fostering music.

How quietly and gently that embryo-echo
Can womb in the bone of a man
And foster across the distance to the mother
A shadow-shelter around this fragile voyage.

Now as you behold your infant, you know
That this child has come from you and to you;
You feel the full force of a father's desire
To protect and shelter.

Perhaps for the first time,
There awakens in you
A sense of your own mortality.

May your heart rest in the grace of the gift
And you sense how you have been called
Inside the dream of this new destiny.

May you be gentle and loving,
Clear and sure.

May you trust in the unseen providence
That has chosen you all to be a family.

May you stand sure on our ground
And know that every grace you need
Will unfold before you
Like all the mornings of your life.[55]

Some credit Leo Durocher, former player and manager, with this quip: "Baseball is like Church. Many attend, few understand." I pray that as you read these pages, especially this chapter, you feel understood, finding peace in the solidarity of this fraternal community.

Only a select few will ever play in a World Series, or see their number retired in the rafters. Most of us are called to the extraordinary tasks of being ordinary—except to our children. To them, we play a leading role. For better or for worse, we are their rock—one that provides a foundation or one that causes bruises.

With each sunrise, we awaken to the daily demands to fill our day which, seen from the perspective of "unseen providence," are indeed blessings. Ask any parent about the emptiness and the silence when their children leave home. How they miss all that noise and inconvenient mess!

In light of the "brightness that surprises your life," we can see in our children what God sees in us. We also appreciate how we carry within us the best of our fathers and mothers, grandfathers and grandmothers. I reflect at times on how I continue not only Grandpa Walters's baseball loyalty, but the kindness and love that he exhibited half a century ago, and his as well as my father's sacrificial love. In that providential brightness not only do I see the external characteristics I have inherited along with my name, I see how my heart has been shaped to love as I have been loved.

In the summer of 2004 my Uncle Tommy, who was more like a grandfather than an uncle, returned from Florida to spend his final months with us. Through the years he and I had watched many games together. A month before he died we watched one more game—a classic between the Red Sox and our beloved Mets—from eighteen years prior. During a family party, while many were eating dessert outside, I went to check on him, knowing how his health was failing. After helping him sip some water, I grabbed the remote to surf the channels until we landed on a replay of game 7 of the 1986 World Series.

As we re-watched the Mets win their second championship, I was moved with emotion as I knew this was going to be the closest he and I could actually come to watching the Mets win it all together. He would transition to the next life that fall, and among the many wonderful memories he created in my life, that one summer night claims a special place.

Each and every day, silently and courageously, innumerable fathers take the field to play the game of life under the watchful eyes of their loved ones. And when all is said and done, when we hang up our jersey after that last game, may we close our eyes, take our last breath, and filled with grateful hearts, find our Creator in that field we all have imagined in our dreams. Then, we will ask our heavenly father, "Is this heaven?" already knowing the answer.

# Conclusion

"It ain't over till it's over."[56]

—Yogi Berra

"All the believers were one in heart and mind."

—Acts 4:32

J esus often went to the desert to pray, to find space and time to reconnect with his Father. For me, my "desert" was Shea Stadium, and then Citi Field, both on the same plot of former swampland in Flushing, Queens.

As a kid—and I thank God I still do today—I attended many games with my dad; we began by sharing fries and progressed to cheering with beers. It was our place to do much more than just take in a game. I also have gone there with friends, with family, with my wife, and now with my kids. I joke that being a Mets fan keeps them (and their old man) humble.

Every season I also try to take in a few games alone. There, I can watch the game, and between innings, the fans. I watch young fathers and mothers and their children grabbing a snack, explaining the rules of the game, and pointing to the big apple in centerfield when the home team collects another long ball.

I watch middle-aged folks sitting beside their aging parents, recalling baseball memories and hoping for one more postseason campaign.

I watch couples who are still learning about and from one another, the awkwardness and the sweetness in their eyes, as they both wonder if this is just the first of their many, many innings of love.

I watch grandparents and their children's children, taking photographs and exchanging smiles and hugs, basking under the outfield sun. While today's stars chase history, they talk of past giants of the game.

Finally, I watch strangers uniting for a few hours. Outside the park they are divided by all that causes schism in our world; inside, they are united as they watch the game that heals.

In 2006, the Mets were playing game 7 of the National League Championship Series against the St. Louis Cardinals. For hours that evening, deep down the first base line in the mezzanine section of my beloved Shea Stadium, I stayed on my feet. You wouldn't dare sit.

In the top of the sixth, the mood was uproarious. The game was tied when Mets left fielder Endy Chavez leaped over the wall to rob Cardinals' third baseman, Scott Rolen, of a two-run homer. Shea went wild. When Chavez made that catch, we found ourselves hugging strangers, leaping over one another because we had just witnessed one of the greatest plays in Mets history. If they could beat the Cardinals and go on to win it all, it might stand as one of the most important catches in baseball history.

Then, in the bottom of the ninth, trailing 3-1, with two out and the bases loaded, the Mets' outfielder Carlos Beltran stood at the plate. One more hit could send the

Mets to the World Series. Instead, Beltran took a wicked curveball from Adam Wainwright for strike three. The Mets lost, but it still gives me chills to think about a moment like the one after Chavez's miraculous catch, when I felt overwhelmed by community and showered by the love of strangers.

Chiara Lubich writes, "Let everything else go, but unity never."[57] Just imagine if we could joyfully live our lives together, not just at historic moments in baseball but within our familial bond as God's children.

When I sit by myself now in the upper deck of Citi Field, moments like that one come back to me. They are reinforced by the community surrounding me, be it a small April crowd, or an intense October night where each pitch weighs just a bit more than the one before. I find peace here.

What if we, as a human family, could unite to celebrate life like we did that day at old Shea Stadium, not just in a crowd of like-minded fans, but wherever the human family is gathered. Imagine a world where we celebrate all of life with the same passion as we do a walk-off home run. Imagine cherishing life, especially the lives of those we do not understand, without judgement and without blame, as we do for our baseball heroes. Imagine uniting around strangers in moments of need, as we do when we find our team a run short with only a few outs left.

Baseball may be just a game, but it reveals what once was and what is still possible.

As a father, or as anyone entrusted with the life of another, I pray you see the blessings in your special vocation. Like the players on the field, there will be times when you are called to sacrifice, others when you are left on the sidelines cheering on your teammates. There will be many at-bats when you play hero, and there will be tough losses when you have to keep lifting the spirits of your companions at home.

I pray you find solidarity with me and with other dads, as you would in a pennant-clinching game 7. You are not alone in this roller coaster of a season; you are loved by God and called each day to reflect that love to those around you. Your relationship with God is fundamental to your privileged vocation. This bit of wisdom is attributed to St. Vincent de Paul: "If God is the center of your life, no words are necessary. Your mere presence will touch hearts." Being in union with God changes everything.

I introduced this book by describing two pilgrimages: to Cooperstown, New York and to the Vatican, places where we remember the greatest in our game and in our faith. I pray you see that greatness in yourself; I invite you each day to be a hero and a legend to all who call you friend, partner, and of course, dad.

Thank you for allowing me to share some of my life with you. As you continue to write your own story, remember that God has called you to your vocation. Ask God for what you need, and with the intercession of St. Joseph, and all the generations of fathers, let us keep stepping up to the plate each day, swinging for the fences, aiming to be the most valuable player in the lives of our children and family.

St. Teresa of Calcutta writes, "Yesterday is gone. Tomorrow has not yet come. We have only today. Let us begin."[58]

Batter up!

# Sources Consulted

Amalie, Benjamin. "An Emotional Day for Bill Buckner." *Boston Globe*, April 8, 2008. https://www.boston.com/sports/articles/2008/04/08/ an_emotional_day_for_bill_buckner/?rss_id=Boston.com+--+Red+Sox+News.

"Baseball Reference: Bill Bucker." https://www.baseball-reference.com/ players/b/bucknbio1.shtml.

Bell, Jillian. "Fertilized Human Egg Emits Microscopic Flash of Light." CBC News. April 27, 2016. https://www.cbc.ca/news/technology/ sperm-egg-zinc-sparks-1.3553550.

Berra, Yogi, *When You Come to a Fork in the Road, Take it!: Inspiration and Wisdom from One of Baseball's Greatest Heroes.* Paris: Hachette Books, 2001.

"Blessed Frédéric Ozanam Biography." Vincentian Formation Network. November 11, 2013. http://vincentians.com/en/blessed-frederic-ozanam-biography-i/.

Brett, George. "There's No Day like Opening Day." MiLB.com. March 18, 2015. https://www.milb.com/news/gcs-113303956.

Brown, Elizabeth A. R. "Authority, the Family, and the Dead in Late Medieval France." *French Historical Studies.* Vol. 16, No.4 (Autumn,1990): 16.

Buechner, Frederick. *Wishful Thinking: A Theological ABC.* London: Collins, 1973.

Clarke, P.J. *Lives That Made a Difference: An RSME Book for Schools.* Durham, NC: Strategic Book Group, 2011.

Day, Dorothy. *The Long Loneliness.* San Francisco: Harper Collins, 1997.

Dickson, Paul. *Baseball Is...Defining the National Pastime.* New York: Dover Publications, 2011.

Duduit. Del. *Dugout Devotions:Inspirational Hits from MLB's Best.* Hoover, AL: Iron Stream Books, 2015.

Fischer, David. *The New York Yankees of the 1950s.* Guilford, CT: Lyons Press, 2019.

Francis. @Pontifex. November 21, 2013. https://twitter.com/pontifex/status/403528682800562176?lang=en.

Francis. @Pontifex. April 25, 2021. https://twitter.com/Pontifex/status/1386253650155163649.

Freud, Sigmund. *Civilization and Its Discontents.* Edited and translated by James Strachey. New York: W. W Norton, 2005.

Gehrig, Lou. "Luckiest Man." National Baseball Hall of Fame. July 4, 1939. https://baseballhall.org/discover-more/stories/baseball-history/lou-gehrig-luckiest-man.

Hoffman, Paul. "July 4, 1939: Lou Gehrig Says Farewell to Baseball with Luckiest Man Speech at Yankee Stadium." https://sabr.org/gamesproj/game/july-4-1939-lou-gehrig-appreciation-day-ruth-and-gehrig-end-feud/.

"If The Only Prayer You Ever Say in Your Whole Life Is 'Thank You,' That Would Suffice." Sounds True. May 22, 2013 https://resources.soundstrue.com/blog/if-the-only-prayer-you-ever-say-in-your-whole-life-is-thank-you-that-would-suffice/.

Keating, Thomas. *Invitation to Love 20th Anniversary Edition: The Way of Christian Contemplation.* London: Bloomsbury Publishing, 2012.

Keating, Thomas. *Divine Therapy and Addiction: Centering Prayer and the Twelve Steps.* Brooklyn: Lantern Books, 2009.

Krell, David. *The New York Yankees in Popular Culture.* Jefferson, NC: McFarland & Company, Inc., 2019.

Lamb, Chris & Ed Henry. "Jackie Robinson's 100th birthday— His faith in God was the secret ingredient to his success." Fox News. January 28, 2019. https://www.foxnews.com/opinion/jackie-robinsons-100th-birthday-his-faith-in-god-was-the-secret-ingredient-to-his-success.

Lubich, Chiara. "Unpublished Diary of June 14, 1968." *A New Way: The Spirituality of Unity.* Hyde Park: New City Press, 2006.

McDonough, Jill. "We're Human Beings." Poetry Foundation, 2012. https://www.poetryfoundation.org/poems/57870/were-human-beings.

Merton, Thomas. *Conjectures of a Guilty Bystander.* New York: Image Books, 1996. 206.

Merton, Thomas. *Contemplative Prayer.* New York: Image Books, 1969.

Merton, Thomas. *The Asian Journal of Thomas Merton.* New York: New Direction Books, 1975.

Mother Teresa. *In the Heart of the World: Thoughts, Stories & Prayers.* Novato, CA: New World Library, 1997.

Nouwen, Henri J.M. *"Being Living Signs of Love."* Henri Nouwen Society, August 9, 2018. *https://henrinouwen.org/meditation/living-signs-love/.*

Nouwen, Henri J.M. *Return of the Prodigal Son: Story of Homecoming.* New York, Doubleday, Reissue Edition, 1994.

Nouwen, Henri J.M. *The Spiritual Life: Eight Essential Titles by Henri Nouwen.* New York: HarperCollins, 2016.

O'Donohue, John. *To Bless the Space Between Us: A Book of Blessings.* New York: Doubleday, 2008.

Ortiz, David. *Big Papi: My Story of Big Dreams and Big Hits.* New York: St. Martin's Griffin, 2007.

Palmer, Parker J. *Let Your Life Speak: Listening for The Voice of Vocation.* San Francisco: John Wiley and Sons Inc., 2000.

Piazza, Mike. "Baseball Hall of Fame Induction Ceremony." ASAP Sports. July 24, 2016. http://www.asapsports.com/show_interview. php?id=121876.

Retrosheet. May 8, 1968. Accessed April 1, 2021. https://www.retrosheet. org/boxesetc/1968/B05080OAK1968.htm.

Reyes, Ernest. "A Brooklyn Dodgers Themed Prayer/Mass Card at LeLands Auction." Dodgers Blue Heaven, May 17, 2016. http://www.dodgersblueheaven.com/2016/05/a-brooklyn-dodgers-themed-prayermass. html.

Rohr, Richard. "Change as a Catalyst for Transformation." June 30, 2016. https://cac.org/change-catalyst-transformation-2016-06-30/.

Rohr, Richard. "Recovering Our Original Unity." Center for Action and Contemplation. November 24, 2020. *https://cac.org/recovering-ouroriginal-unity-2020-11-24/.*

Rohr, Richard. *The Universal Christ: How a Forgotten Reality Can Change Everything We See, Hope for and Believe.* New York: Convergent Books, 2019.

Ruth, Babe. In "Famous Quotes | Babe Ruth." Baberuth.com. 2019. http:// www.baberuth.com/quotes/.

Scott-Maxwell, Florida. *The Measure of My Days.* New York: Norton, 1986.

Skipper, John C. *A Biographical Dictionary of Major League Baseball Managers.* Jefferson: McFarland, 2003.

Tertullian, *Apologia. De Spectaculis.* London: Harvard University Press, 1953.

Tolle, Eckhart. *The Power of Now.* Vancouver: Namaste Publishing, 1999.

Torres, Maria. "How Brad Ausmus Used Advanced Data to Spur Justin Verlander's Career." *Los Angeles Times,* May 6, 2019. https://www.latimes.com/sports/angels/la-sp-angels-brad-ausmus-justin-verlanderdetroit-tigers-manager-analytics-20190506-story.html.

Tzu, Lao. *Tao Te Ching,* Chapter 15. http://thetaoteching.com/taoteching15.html.

Van Esselstyn, Drew. "The Time of His Life." Fellowship of Christian Athletes. April 30, 2018. https://www.fca.org/fca-in-action/2018/04/30/the-time-of-his-life.

Williams, Pat, and Mike Sielski. *How to Be Like Jackie Robinson: Life Lessons from Baseball's Greatest Hero.* Deerfield Beach, FL: Health Communications, Inc., 2005.

Williams, Ted. *The Cooperstown Symposium on Baseball and American Culture, 1999.* Jefferson, NC: McFarland, 2000.

# Notes

1.  "Blessed Frédéric Ozanam Biography," Vincentian Formation Network, November 11, 2013, http://vincentians.com/en/blessed-frederic-ozanam-biography-i/.

2.  Clayton Kershaw, in Drew Van Esselstyn, "The Time of His Life," Fellowship of Christian Athletes, April 30, 2018, https://www.fca.org/fca-in-action/2018/04/30/the-time-of-his-life.

3.  "Message of Pope Francis for the 51st World Day of Prayer for Vocations" (2014), 3, https://www.vatican.va/content/francesco/en/messages/vocations/documents/papa-francesco_20140115_51-messaggio-giornata-mondiale-vocazioni.html.

4.  Chris Lamb and Ed Henry, "Jackie Robinson's 100th birthday—His Faith in God Was the Secret Ingredient to His Success," Fox News, January 28, 2019, https://www.foxnews.com/opinion/jackie-robinsons-100th-birthday-his-faith-in-god-was-the-secret-ingredient-to-his-success.

5.  Ernest Reyes, "A Brooklyn Dodgers Themed Prayer/Mass Card at LeLands Auction," Dodgers Blue Heaven, May 17, 2016, http://www.dodgersblueheaven.com/2016/05/a-brooklyn-dodgers-themed-prayermass.html.

6.  Parker J. Palmer, *Let Your Life Speak: Listening for The Voice of Vocation* (San Francisco: John Wiley and Sons Inc., 2000), 4-5.

7.  Frederick Buechner, *Wishful Thinking: A Theological ABC* (London: Collins, 1973), 95.

8.  Henri J.M. Nouwen, "Being Living Signs of Love," Henri Nouwen Society, August 9, 2018. *https://henrinouwen.org/meditation/living-signs-love/.*

9.  Richard Rohr and Joseph Martos, *From Wild Man to Wise Man: Reflections on Male Spirituality* (Cincinnati: Franciscan Media, 2005), 1.

10. Mike Piazza, "Baseball Hall of Fame Induction Ceremony," ASAP Sports. July 24, 2016. http://www.asapsports.com/show_interview.php?id=121876.

11. Francis, @Pontifex, April 25, 2021, https://twitter.com/Pontifex/status/1386253650155163649.

12. Ben Zobrist, in Del Duduit, *Dugout Devotions: Inspirational Hits from MLB's Best* (Hoover, AL: Iron Stream Books, 2015), 13.

13. Babe Ruth, "Famous Quotes | Babe Ruth," Baberuth.com. 2019, http://www.baberuth.com/quotes/.

14. Dorothy Day, *The Long Loneliness* (San Francisco: Harper Collins, 1997), 243.

15. "Retrosheet," May 8, 1968. https://www.retrosheet.org/boxesetc/1968/B05080OAK1968.htm.

16. Chiara Lubich, *A New Way: The Spirituality of Unity* (Hyde Park: New City Press, 2006), 49.

17. Gehrig, Lou, "Luckiest Man," National Baseball Hall of Fame, July 4, 1939. https://baseballhall.org/discover-more/stories/baseball-history/lou-gehrig-luckiest-man.

18. Richard Rohr. "Recovering Our Original Unity," Center for Action and Contemplation, November 24, 2020. *https://cac.org/recovering-our-original-unity-2020-11-24/*.

19. Thomas Merton, *The Asian Journal of Thomas Merton* (New York: New Direction Books, 1975), 318–319.

20. Eckhart Tolle, *The Power of Now* (Vancouver: Namaste Publishing, 1999), 33.

21. Jillian Bell, "Fertilized Human Egg Emits Microscopic Flash of Light," CBC News, April 27, 2016, https://www.cbc.ca/news/technology/sperm-egg-zinc-sparks-1.3553550.

22. Tommy Lasorda, in Paul Dickson, *Baseball Is...Defining the National Pastime* (New York: Dover Publications, 2011), 148.

23. Chiara Lubich, "Unpublished Diary of June 14, 1968," *A New Way*, 118.

24. Lady Julian of Norwich, in Richard Rohr, *The Universal Christ: How a Forgotten Reality can Change Everything We See, Hope for and Believe* (New York: Convergent Books, 2019), 69.

25. Florida Scott-Maxwell, *The Measure of My Days* (New York: Norton, 1986), 42.

26. Andrew McCutchen, in Duduit, 30.

27. Maria Torres, "How Brad Ausmus Used Advanced Data to Spur Justin Verlander's Career," *Los Angeles Times*, May 6, 2019, https://www.latimes.com/sports/angels/la-sp-angels brad-ausmus-justin-verlander-detroit-tigers-manager-analytics-20190506-story.html.

28. Richard Rohr, "Change as a Catalyst for Transformation," June 30, 2016, https://cac.org/change-catalyst-transformation-2016-06-30/.

29. Henri J. M. Nouwen, *The Spiritual Life: Eight Essential Titles by Henri Nouwen* (New York: HarperCollins, 2016), 7.

30. Thomas Keating, *Invitation to Love 20th Anniversary Edition: The Way of Christian Contemplation* (London: Bloomsbury Publishing, 2012), 57.

31. Francisco Lindor, in Duduit, 21-22.
32. Thomas Merton, *Conjectures of a Guilty Bystander* (New York: Image Books, 1996), 206.
33. George Brett, in "There's No Day like Opening Day." MiLB.com. March 18, 2015, https://www.milb.com/news/gcs-113303956.
34. Meister Eckhart, in "If The Only Prayer You Ever Say In Your Whole Life Is 'Thank You,' That Would Suffice," Sounds True, May 22, 2013, https://resources.soundstrue.com/blog/if-the-only-prayer-you-ever-say-in-your-whole-life-is-thank-you-that-would-suffice/.
35. Tertullian et al., *Tertullian: Apology: De Spectaculis* (London: W. Heinemann, 1953), 39, 7.
36. Casey Stengel, in David Fischer, *The New York Yankees of the 1950s* (Guilford, CT: Lyons Press, 2019), 1.
37. 38 Richard Rohr, *The Universal Christ*, 207.
38. P.J. Clarke, *Lives That Made a Difference: An RSME Book for Schools* (Durham, NC:Eloquent Books, 2011), 219.
39. David Ortiz, *Big Papi: My Story of Big Dreams and Big Hits* (New York: St. Martin's Griffin, 2007), 18.
40. Sigmund Freud, *Civilization and its Discontents*, in J. Strachey, ed. and trans., *The Standard Edition of the Complete Psychological Works of Sigmund Freud* (London: Hogarth Press, originally published 1930), 47.
41. Henri J.M. Nouwen, *Return of the Prodigal Son: Story of Homecoming* (New York, Doubleday, Reissue Edition, 1994), 20.
42. John C. Skipper, *A Biographical Dictionary of Major League Baseball Managers* (Jefferson NC, McFarland, 2011), 12.
43. The Cooperstown Symposium on Baseball and American Culture, 1999 (Jefferson, NC: McFarland: 2000), 141.
44. "Baseball Reference: Bill Bucker," https://www.baseballreference.com/players/b/bucknbio1.shtml.
45. Benjamin Amalie, "An Emotional Day for Bill Buckner," *Boston Globe*, April 8, 2008, https://www.boston.com/sports/articles/2008/04/08/an_emotional_day_for_bill_buckner/?rss_id=Boston.com+--+Red+Sox+News.
46. Yogi Berra, in David Krell, *The New York Yankees in Popular Culture* (Jefferson, NC: McFarland & Company, Inc., 2019), 193.
47. Francis, @Pontifex, November 21, 2013, https://twitter.com/pontifex/status/403528682800562176?lang=en.
48. Lao-Tzu. *"Tao Te Ching"* Chapter 15.
49. Keating, 3.
50. Keating, 63.

51. Thomas Merton, *Contemplative Prayer* (New York: Image Books, 1969), 67.

52. Paul Hoffman, "July 4,1939: Lou Gehrig Says Farewell to Baseball with Luckiest Man Speech at Yankee Stadium," https://sabr.org/gamesproj/game/july-4-1939-lou-gehrig-appreciation-day-ruth-and-gehrig-end-feud/.

53. Pat Williams and Mike Sielski, *How to Be Like Jackie Robinson: Life Lessons from Baseball's Greatest Hero* (Deerfield Beach, FL: Health Communications, Inc., 2005), 17.

54. Jill McDonough, "We're Human Beings," Poetry Foundation, 2012, https://www.poetryfoundation.org/poems/57870/were-human-beings.

55. John O'Donohue, *To Bless the Space Between Us: A Book of Blessings* (Doubleday: New York, 2008), 82.

56. Yogi Berra, *When You Come to a Fork in the Road, Take It!: Inspiration and Wisdom from One of Baseball's Greatest Heroes* (Paris: Hachette Books, 2001), 88.

57. Chiara Lubich, *A New Way*, 55.

58. Mother Teresa, *In the Heart of the World: Thoughts, Stories & Prayers* (Novato, California: New World Library, 1997), 17.